written by
Kate McKinnon
Christina Vandervlist

illustrations
Christina Vandervlist
Dustin Wedekind
Jean Power

photography
Kate McKinnon
Jeroen Medema
Kyle Cassidy

created with
Jean Power
Christina Vandervlist
Dustin Wedekind
Gabriella van Diepen

3

Contemporary Geometric Beadwork

is produced & published by Kate McKinnon Design
copyright 2012 Kate McKinnon

www.katemckinnon.com

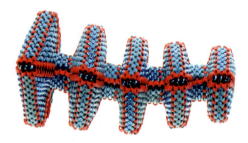

All rights reserved. No part of this publication or associated eBook may be reproduced or transmitted by any means, electronic or mechanical, without direct permission from the author. No portion of this book may be taught or copied and distributed as class handouts without the direct permission of both the author and the project designer. In many cases, the contributors to this book teach beadwork for a living, and are willing, excited and available to come to your area and teach for your Guild, Bead Society, private group or bead store.

We encourage you to explore the ideas within our pages, and make your own journey. If you develop work based on our ideas or our patterns, we would appreciate it if you credit the designer. If you submit pieces to magazines or books, or teach professionally, the same applies.

We are very interested in related work, and would love to include your own well-made, original expressions of geometric beadwork in our interactive eBook version of *Contemporary Geometric Beadwork*, and also for future volumes. Submit photos to us at cgb@katemckinnon.com.

Please contact us with any questions or errors; we would appreciate the opportunity to clarify or correct the text in the electronic version. This book was entirely printed and bound in the United States by Jostens Publishing, www.jostens.com.

ISBN 978-0-9816468-0-0

This book was inspired by and is dedicated to the glorious beady bodies of work created by Jean Power and Dustin Wedekind, and was helped to fruition by the clever hands and nimble mind of Christina Vandervlist. I am indebted to each of them, and to every person who beaded, questioned, illustrated, and wrote to us.

The scope of this project would not have been possible without the generosity of spirit (and the pre-orders) of the hundreds of people who participated, freely sharing their ideas, their colourways, their patterns, and their love of the tiny glass marvels that captivate us all.

... beads, how we love them ...

For the full Team Acknowledgements, please see pgs 230-231.
All photographs by Kate McKinnon unless otherwise noted.

Table Of Contents

9	Introduction
12	Basics
14	Supplies
20	Tips & Terminology
26	Sizing & Closures
28	Simple Flat Square
30	Warped Square
34	Bellybands
38	RAW Band
39	MRAW Band
40	Double Bands
42	Zigged Bands

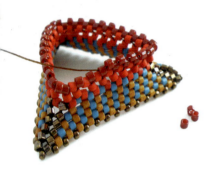

44	Triangles
46	Flat Peyote Triangle
56	Turning Triangles into Puffs
62	Power Puff Ring & Bezel
68	Power Puff Bangle
70	Caldera Bangle
79	Finishing Geometric Bangles
82	Pyramids & Tetrahedrons
88	Hidden Clasp

92	Wings and Horns
100	Tri-Wing Ring
108	Many-Wing Bangles
110	Decreasing or Tailoring Wings
112	Turning Wings Into Horns
114	Tinyhorn Bangle with Removable Bellyband
120	Horned Melon Bangle
126	Turquoise Hornwing
128	Golden-Horned Sea Serpent

136 **Zigs and Zags**

138   Double Rick Rack Bangle
150   Horned Rick-Rack
156   Zigged Parrot Tulips
161   More MRAW Flowers

164 **Glorious Combinations**

164   Fortuneteller Bangle
196   Helix Bangle
202   Triple Helix
209   Helix Sketch in 8° Rounds
214   Jalisco Bangle

216 **Cones**

218   Basic Cone
224   DoubleCone Rings and
           other Coned Delights

230 **Team Acknowledgements**

232 **Introduction for Backwards Readers**
     (Or Backwards Beaders)

236 **Bead Number Tables**

"...I know nothing with any certainty, but
the sight of the stars makes me dream."

Vincent van Gogh

Contemporary Geometric Beadwork by Kate McKinnon   7

Photos, previous pages:

Cover: Horned Bangle, Rayo Boursier
Space Pod Fortuneteller Bangle, JoAnn Baumann

Page 2: Fortuneteller Bangle, Kat Oliva

Page 4: Power Puff Rope Swatch, Dustin Wedekind

Page 5: Power Puff Bangle, Jean Power, Photo by Kyle Cassidy
Funnelweb discs, Dustin Wedekind

Table of Contents:
Helix Bracelet, Julie Glasser
Tri Wing Ring in process, Kate McKinnon
Flat Peyote Triangle, Kate McKinnon
Horned Melon Bangle, Kim Boeckman

Rick-Rack Bangle, Leslie Venturoso, photo by Leslie
DoubleCone Ring, Charlotte Aziz, photo by Charlotte
Lairy Caldera, Kirsty Little, photo by Kirsty

Above: Two Fortuneteller Bangles, stacked:
  Green, Laurel Kubby
  Missoni 77, multicoloured, Susan Mattison

Back Cover: Rick-Rack Bangle, Suzanne Golden

Introduction

This book has been a year and a half in the making, and many fascinating characters have cycled in and out of the project. It started in the summer of 2011, with a *Seed Bead Summit* at the Atomic Ranch in Tucson. Beaders attending were Dustin Wedekind, Marcia DeCoster, Jean Power, Gabriella van Diepen, Jeroen Medema, and Teresa Sullivan. Christina Vandervlist came on board in 2012.

We didn't know what we were up to, but I had an idea about a community project, something that would go beyond the project books and get to the heart of what sorts of soaring shapes were possible. We had these huge towering ideas, ideas that barely fit into our heads, and I wanted to show them in forms that engaged beginners and advanced beaders alike. Our goal as a team was to encourage people to dive fearlessly into complex pieces, to realize that yes, absolutely, they could make them.

We asked basic questions about old starts, and old questions about new forms, and we came up with a simple band structure that knocked our own socks off. We built Wings and watched them turn into Horns, we Zigged our groovy Bellyband for a simple Rick-Rack in one pass, and we said to ourselves, again and again, "Why in the heck didn't we do this before?"

We kept going, seeing what we could make, and we built cathedrals and Points and corners and cantilevers in a fabric of glass, brick by glittering brick, and beaders of the world came right along with us. We hope you enjoy the lines and the starts and the jumps and the leaps, and that they inspire you to create new forms of your own, and especially to go beyond our patterns.

The *Contemporary Geometric Beadwork* project is much larger than this book alone: it encompasses an ongoing body of work being created all over the world. The companion eBook is alive, with glittering photographs, video, and constantly updating content, the online galleries will continue to grow, and the second paper volume is already underway.

Learn more at www.ContemporaryGeometricBeadwork.com and keep in touch with me at www.katemckinnon.com. And thank you for your support of our work and this exciting project.

Love and beads,
Kate

Purple Prose

Watch for purple words and phrases throughout the book, as they tell you that there is more to find on that topic. In the paper book, you will find more about highlighted terms either in the Basics section or in the Table of Contents.

In the eBook, you will find that there are even more colours, and each of them are clickable, and take you to more photographs, patterns, information, galleries, or to the artist's personal web sites or online shops, or perhaps to a bead store, magazine article, or indexed reference. We are excited to offer you these worlds within worlds and will continue to add to the online resources as new work appears and time permits.

Don't forget your sense of play and adventure as you explore our ideas. Most of our discoveries were made by happenstance, as we followed some idea down a winding lane. We are happy to be distracted by sunbeams, stray thoughts and sounds from over the hill. How else would we evolve? As Roger Von Oech says,

"Most people think of success and failure as opposites, but they both are products of the same process...It's important for the explorer to be willing to be led astray."

Below: Two Tri-Wing Rings by Dustin Wedekind and Kate McKinnon

Opposite: Photo of Gabriella van Diepen (and our oh-so-wearable bangles) by Kyle Cassidy. These shots were taken in Sabino Canyon, in Kate's home town of Tucson, Arizona, with a crew that included (in addition to Gabri, Kate and Kyle) Jean Power (our style mistress), Emma Bull (our severely overqualified grip) and Jeroen Medema (our lightmaster). Bangles on Gabriella's arm by Jean and Gabri.

"Space is the breath of art."

Frank Lloyd Wright

Basics

"If there is a problem you can't solve, then there is an easier problem you *can* solve: find it."

George Pólya

12 Contemporary Geometric Beadwork by Kate McKinnon

Yes You Can!

At first glance, *Contemporary Geometric Beadwork* may not look like a book meant for beginning beaders, but that doesn't mean that beginners can't make the work. It's all rather straightforward, as most of the pieces are based on just a few structures: a great Bellyband, a simple triangle, a flat square, a few herringbone-style increases and decreases.

Anyone with decent vision (or a good pair of reading glasses) and a love of small handiwork can pick up a needle and beading thread and start off with a Basic Flat Square, or a Flat Peyote Triangle, and then maybe a Tri-Wing Ring.

For very basic basics, and to learn more stitches and techniques that can be used to build or embellish your work, we encourage you to explore the world of the beading magazines. They teach useful stitches and have beginning projects in every issue, and many of them also have lists of bead stores and bead shows in your area. Please also see the Team Pages (230-231) to discover great beginner-level beading and pattern books by Dustin Wedekind and Jean Power.

Below: a Power Puff Ring (pg. 62) by Carol Taylor and a Flat Peyote Triangle (pg. 50) by Kate.

Opposite page, from top: a Flat Peyote Triangle by Kate, a Möbius Double-Cone Ring (pg. 225) by Christina Vandervlist, and a Fortuneteller Bangle (pgs. 164-195) by Christina Porter.

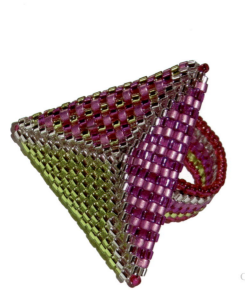

Basics: Supplies

Getting Started

You don't need much in your toolbox to start beading. You'll want a pack or two of needles (they bend and break with use and need replacing), beading thread, something to cut the thread cleanly (we use things like little sharp scissors and snips) and a few different kinds of beads.

We'll tell you our favorite things, but the world is stuffed with choices and each product has its fans. Admittedly we have strong feelings, but that's only because we are passionate and nerdly people, incapable of ambivalence.

Thread

For the core crew of this book, the thread of choice is definitely Nymo B or D from the cone. It's old school, we know, but it's what we like. Nymo is a lush, sturdy nylon Italian upholstery thread, and it comes in a variety of weights and colours. It has a positive "hand", it means business, it feels like silk and needs no waxing. But this heavenly Nymo of which we speak only rolls off of the large cones.

The little paper bobbins of Nymo (which are sold in almost every bead store) are conveniently sized for travel but the thread is uncoated and is really *nothing* like the cone thread. If you only know Nymo from a bobbin, you don't know Nymo. And if you use the bobbins, plan on waxing. Most beaders love the little containers of microcrystalline or synthetic wax but some are old school and have actual beeswax.

Other threads used by beaders who contributed to this book are KO, Sono, One G, CLon, Fireline, Silamide, and Power Pro. Try them all, and see what suits you. Thread choice is a personal and important element in your beadwork. Don't even *think* of letting us tell you what to do.

Thread As A Secondary Structure

If you're using any single ply unpierceable thread, your product of choice can't easily be used to weave a secondary structure inside your work.

Unpierceable thread (such as Fireline) holds the beads together by their holes; their fates are the same and they make a single structure. Many beaders prefer unpierceable thread, and there are certainly applications for which it's perfect. For the beadwork in this book, however, we chose Nymo from the cone because it *can* be pierced, which means that we can use it to weave our little strong-webs inside the beads.

Doing this, working like weavers, moving through previously placed threads as we place our new stitches, we can make a robust secondary structure inside the beadwork, creating a fabric that resembles a linen weave. This enhances our tailoring, giving us both a hidden support structure that we can rely on to take some of the pressure off of the beads, and something to sew into besides the bead holes. (You can imagine how handy it is to have both the bead holes and the fabric of the thread weave when sewing on snaps, buttons, or embellishment.

Because of the way it's made, of joined fiber strands, Nymo has a grain. It's really much like your hair; ideally, you don't want to rub it backwards. If you can't tell which end you are on by gently running it through your fingers, thread the end that comes off of the spool first, and you'll always be right. This grain also means that the thread tends to felt itself together as you pierce it, and backing out mistakes can be very difficult.

Remember to think kindly of the thread as you pull your needle through the beads. Pull the needle straight out of the bead holes, so that the thread isn't pulled across the bead edges. If a length of thread goes bad, and begins fraying, fuzzing or tearing, simply weave it in and start a new one.

Simple hair ties, beer can cozies and produce nets come in handy to keep the thread neat on our large spools.

Contemporary Geometric Beadwork by Kate McKinnon

Basics: Supplies

Needles

Needle preference has a lot to do with hand size and dexterity. Most of us on the CGB crew prefer needles in size 11 or 12, 2" long. Beading needles are inexpensive enough for you to experiment with– we recommend that you try them all and choose the ones most comfortable for your fingers. Kate swears by Size 11 Pony needles, 2" long, from India, and Christina prefers the John James #12 shorts.

An interesting fact about needles is that their eye-holes are punched. This means that one side is rough, and one smooth. If you are having a hard time threading a needle, turn the eye over and try again.

When we thread our needle, we are really needling our thread. We pinch the thread (which we have likely licked) between our finger and thumb, and slide the eye of the needle down on top of it. Try it!

To Knot Or Not

For a variety of reasons having to do with tailoring, lumps and bumps, most of Team CGB don't knot. Whenever possible, we prefer to weave threads in (or out) when beginning or ending. Be sure to leave little tails when you weave in or out, and don't cut them until you are finished working in those sections. We very much like Valerie Hector's suggestion of using a removable stop bead on all new threads, not just when you start a new piece.

When weaving in a thread, try to follow the existing thread path as much as possible to avoid distorting your beadwork in unpredictable and possibly undesirable ways. As long as you change direction at least twice, the thread will be securely anchored. If you are using unpierceable thread, you may have a deeper need to knot. Make your decision based on your materials.

Visible Thread is Vulnerable Thread

Whenever possible minimize your thread exposure. If it's necessary to use thread to attach another element, such as a soldered metal ring or a clasp, make a loop that gives the ring room to move, and consider covering it with tiny beads that cover your thread (see Tetrahedrons, pg. 87, for an example). We try never to leave thread exposed on the edges of our work, whether flat or dimensional.

Work Surface

Some people enjoy beading on synthetic bead mats, because they are foldable, lightweight and tend to hold the beads in place. They can be used on cookie sheets, put in stacking trays, or laid out on beach sand. Christina swears by them. Below, you can see a shot of her setup while she was beading our first Fortuneteller Bangle. Note the beads neatly sorted into piles, the perfectly neat work field. (Those of us with messy trays say, "Snork!")

Dustin beads from a shallow wooden bowl, like a shaman reading water or mixing herbs. All of the beads are together, and he fishes the one he wants out of the bowl with his needle. Marcia DeCoster mixes her beads together as well, and she says it gives her a better feel for the colourway to let the beads play on the tray as well as in the piece in progress.

Kate loves to have neat little piles of beads but always ends up with a scatter of sparkle across her purple velvet board. Teresa Sullivan only likes to work on white plates with a bit of curve. Sandy Wogaman likes a watercolour tray (devilled egg servers are good too) to keep her beads separate. Both Kate and Cath Thomas like to work in stackable trays, which can be quickly moved out of the way without disturbing the projects in process, or stacked to the rafters when we find that we are working on twenty things at once. Jean Power can work anywhere, on anything, and use any thread, but if we were all Jean Power, the universe would explode, and so the rest of us get by.

For travel, we love the aluminum tins that snap securely together. They come with synthetic pads, but any sort of custom pad or covered board can be used. See our online Resources section for where to buy real velvet pads, stacking trays, and travel tins. Find the synthetic pads at any bead store.

Basics: Supplies

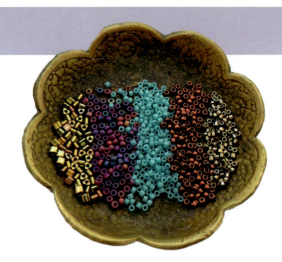

Right: Each of these beads is marked 11°, but you can see how different they are in shape and girth.

Seed Beads

Seed beads are little glass marvels in a doughnut shape. The ones you see in bead shops usually hail from the Czech Republic, India, or Japan, and are found in many sizes. For the work in this book, we used them in sizes 8° and 11° for beadwork and 13° and 15° for edging, embellishing and tailoring.

Japanese seed beads are very even and work well for precision patterns. Czech and Indian seed beads are made with looser sizing standards and different equipment, and they vary both in dimension and hole size. We mix it up, and use Japanese seed beads where consistency is desirable, and Czech seed beads where texture is more appealing. Czech and Indian seed beads are often sold by the hank, and Japanese beads are packaged loose.

Cylinder Beads

Cylinder beads are even more miraculous in the world of glassworks. The cylinder beads used in this book were all made in Japan, and are incredibly precise and predictable. They have thinner walls than seed beads, which means larger centre holes and more room for thread passes.

Beading is ancient, but precision cylinder beads are new, only having arrived in America in the 1980s. We're the first generation of beady humans to have the opportunity to work with them, and we think about that with happiness and humility. It's a privilege to have these exquisite materials.

The most common size is 11°, although the 10° is gaining in popularity. The 15° can be very fragile, and the holes are much smaller, which make pieces like Lia Melia's (pg. 45) all the more astounding. We used cylinder beads from Toho (Aikos and Treasures) and Miyuki (Delicas) in the making of this book. We do tend to avoid the silk-finished cylinder beads, as they are so fragile.

Crystals and Fire Polished Beads

Leaded glass crystals are extra sparkly, and we use them to emphasize structure or provide an attractive embellishment (see A.J. Reardon's Power Puff Bangle, which features them at every Point Round, pg. 55).

Fire-polished faceted Czech glass beads are also very pretty, and have nice soft holes. (This matters- if you like to use fiber thread, sharp-edged beads and crystals can damage it.)

Swarovski makes leaded crystal beads in many sizes and shapes; the most commonly used are faceted round or bicone shapes. These are usually measured by the millimetre, through the centre of the bead from the entrance hole to the exit hole.

Accent Beads

Gemstone daggers and round gemstone balls make appearances in pieces like the Jalisco Bangle, by Cath Thomas (pg. 214), and glass drop beads appear on various Rick-Rack Bangles, Wing- and Horn-tips. You'll see glass triangle beads show up in MRAW Bellybands, and you may see dichroic Aiko cylinders (look closely in Kate's *Sea Monster* (pg. 99) or Jeannette Cook's fantastic *Triangles* (pg. 90).

You'll see rivolis (flattish crystals with no holes) pop up in bezels, as in Marcia DeCoster's Puff Bezel (pg. 63) and in Jeannette's pendant. There is no bead that we do not love, that we do not contemplate with the eye of a crow and a seamstress.

Right: An assortment of larger seed beads, crystals, fire polished Czech glass, glass daggers, gemstones, handmade glass and rivolis in various sizes. The world is simply stuffed with beads! Isn't it wonderful?

Basics: Tips & Terminology

Bead Breakers

A bead breaker can be as simple as a slender pushpin and an eraser, a low-tech solution to that awkward pair where you meant to add just one, or find a bead in the wrong place. The pushpin tip goes into the bead and explodes it outwards from pressure (preserving your thread from sharp bead shards) and the eraser catches the tip of the pushpin before you donate blood to the project.

The excellent thing about Japanese puzzle erasers (besides how adorable they are) is that they come apart, giving you lots of little shapes to get into tight spaces in your beadwork. The strawberries even have little handles. So cute.

Corners and Side Spaces

When building a geometric shape, corners are created by adding increases to the structure. Any space in your beadwork can be filled with 1, 2 or 3 beads, depending on the effect desired. Any increase or decrease will create a corner, even if begun in the middle of a side.

You can see this in the photo at left; one side of our starting Bellyband has had three increases added to it, forming a triangular opening on that side. The other side of the Band remains blissfully unaware of the disruption and remains round.

Side spaces are where the structure takes on a solid, fabric-like appearance, building a single bead at a time. As you add increases to the corners of a piece, the number of side beads required will grow. In related news, when you are decreasing, the number of side beads will diminish.

Counting

Geometric beadwork has so many aspects that it can be hard to be sure we are talking about the same thing when we say "Round 5" or "five beads per side".

In the illustration at upper right, you can see the variety of ways to count to Round 5. When teaching, we focus on the toothlike appearance of the bead edges (we call them Toothrows), suggesting that students count the teeth rather than the spaces.

When decreasing a geometric shape, the most straightforward way to define size is to count the working beads remaining per side (i.e., decrease down to two beads per side, as illustrated, right).

Guide Round

A Guide Round (or Row) refers to a run of beads woven on top of existing beadwork, providing either a point from which to add more structure or embellishment or a place to run a secondary support structure, such as memory wire (see the Sea Serpent, pg. 128). This sort of an add is also sometimes referred to as "stitching in the ditch".

Guide Rounds are best added in structurally sound areas, and they are easiest to add early in the beading process while the work is narrow and pliant. It may become difficult to reach the area required, or find room in the beads for your needle, when work on the main structure nears completion. Below, a Guide Round added to the lower run of beads in the starting RAW band.

Below: Kate put two Guide Rounds of lovely fat bronze 11° rounds on her Mermaid Cuff. Those rounds could have supported more structure, but currently hold only a pass each of hot red 13° rounds.

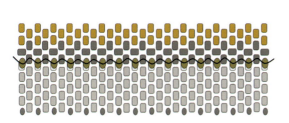

Contemporary Geometric Beadwork by Kate McKinnon

Basics: Tips & Terminology

Herringbone Increase & Decrease

Increase
To create a herringbone increase in your peyote work, simply place 2 beads where there would otherwise be 1 bead, as we do to increase the Simple Flat Triangle, right.

By stacking the pairs of beads on top of one another you will form a rib, which can be continued up and out to build a tip, a corner, a Wing, or a Horn.

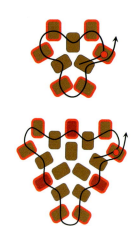

Decrease
A decrease is a stitch taken while adding no beads. You can see this in the illustrations to the right, shown both in flat work and in a decreasing Power Puff Triangle.

Decreases, like Step Ups, can be hard to spot when you are learning, but in reality they are predictable, and the key to spotting them is to study the structure, so that you understand what your rounds *should* be making. That way, if things seem wrong, you can stop and ask yourself why. (And start counting teeth.)

decrease in flat work

corner decreases in circular work

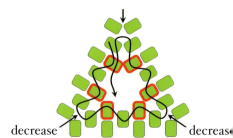

decrease decrease

Needle Back or Needle To

If we tell you to "needle" somewhere, we mean for you to pass your needle through the beadwork (following the existing thread path if possible) to reach a specific point, where presumably the next excitement will begin.

If we tell you to "Needle Up", then we are probably inviting you to either a bead party or to go to acupuncture with us. Either way, say yes!

Pass Through and Pass Back Through

"Passing Through" refers to going once more through a bead you've been through previously. Sometimes this will be done to complete a stitch (see Step Up, pg. 25), while other times it may be required to move through your beadwork to the point necessary to begin the next step.

Above: Passing Through a few beads to get to a new starting point.

Below: Passing Back Through to create a fringe.

We can't say why you want to start your next round one space forward in the illo at upper right, but we bet you have a good reason. Perhaps you are adding a little picot edge to a cute Tri-Wing Ring, as in the one peeking onto the page. To do that, you need to add a few beads, pass through a few beads.

"Pass Back Through" is to pass your needle back through one or more beads that you have passed through previously, this time in the opposite direction. It is often used to create a fringe (right) or add accents to an otherwise complete section of beadwork.

Toothrow

You know that it pains us to have "Toothrow" out of alphabetical order. But perhaps it helps make the point that a Toothrow can be anywhere. Anywhere! When we speak of a Toothrow, what we mean is any peyote or RAW edge; any row or round of beadwork that presents in little teeth, waiting to hook on to something.

When you add a Guide Round or Row to a piece, what you are really doing is sticking a Toothrow onto it, a place for new beadwork to land.

Don't the peyote edges look like little teeth?

23

Basics: Tips & Terminology

Point and Fill Rounds

A Point Round is added by stitching a single bead into each corner, as in the illustration to the right.

A Fill Round of one bead per space follows a Point Round. Fill Rounds may be followed with a Decrease (0 beads in the corner), an Increase (2 beads in the corner), or another Point Round (1 bead). Alternating Point and Fill Rounds is how to continue beading at the same diameter, to make a tube or add depth.

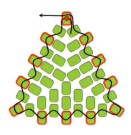

A Point Round

An Increasing Triangle

Point Round added

Fill Round added

If you look at the last drawing on the right, above, and think of the Fill Round as creating little flaps you can pull in, you will see how making tube or decreasing works. Can you see how the adds make three little blue sides to fold straight up (for tube) or fold over and in (to mimic the last Increase Round) and make a Power Puff?

Rows and Rounds

Rows are how we talk about progressions in flat work, and Rounds describe circular work. Rows start and end on opposite sides of your beadwork. Rounds start and finish at the same point.

Many of the pieces in this book can either be worked flat or in the round, but we generally discuss it in terms of Rounds.

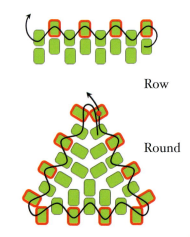

Row

Round

Step Up

To Step Up in peyote stitch, place your final bead of the current round, pass through the first bead from the previous round, and pass through the first bead placed in the current round. This bumps you up on top of the work, and puts you in position to begin the next round.

Regular Step Ups in both flat and circular peyote stitch

Usually you will pass through the first single bead added on the current round. If your increase falls in a corner, or where you have made an increase, you will pass through only the first bead of however many you added.

You will note in the Simple Flat Square (pg. 28) that you pass through the first bead of the corner-placed triplet, and in a corner increase, as shown at right, you pass through into the middle of the two beads.

Skipping the Step Up

If you place the final bead of your round and skip passing through the bead from the previous round, and instead choose to pass immediately through the first bead placed in the current round, you will transform the work from circular to spiral.

Skipping the Step Up

Hidden Step Up

A step up can be difficult to see if it falls where your bead count changes, such as a decrease (see illustration at right). If you need to step up in this situation, remember that if the pair of beads was placed or passed through *in one move*, they must be treated as a single entity for the step up, and you will need to pass through both beads to finish the round.

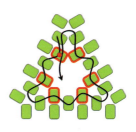

Hidden Step Up

Contemporary Geometric Beadwork by Kate McKinnon

Basics: Sizing & Closures

Bangle sizers and mandrels come in very handy when measuring beadwork, but frankly, even with our combined century of beading experience, sizing 3-d work is still a matter of chance. You must experiment, and test your bead combinations.

Sizing

Sizing beadwork is an art. Each bead or type of bead is unique, and the bead finish drastically affects its girth. People's working tension varies widely; and loose or tight work can mean the difference of an entire size.

Our best advice to you is:

- Work snugly. Don't leave any loose thread, or space between beads. Pull your thread in closely after every stitch, and control your beadwork so that it isn't loose in your hand. Tighter work is more predictable.

- Get a real bangle sizer. What this can measure is not just the beadwork, but what your hand can wiggle into. You can find them in some bead shops, or online. See our online resources section for tips on where to find one, or search the web for "metal bracelet sizer" or "bangle sizer".

- Be flexible. If you make a ring that is slightly bigger or smaller than hoped, you likely have something close to ten fingers, and happily you probably have friends with fingers too. If you happen to make a Zigged Band (pg. 42) that turns out to be too small for your hand, make it into a knockout MRAW Flower (pg. 161). Experiment by making maquettes like rings.

- Try other beads. If you are locked into a size range, like the number of Points in a Helix, and you need it half a Point bigger, add in a coated bead. If it's just a snitch too big, perhaps a matte bead would have been just enough smaller...

- Make Removable Bellybands. Especially a Zigged One. Once you nail your size, you can make as many bangles off of the Band as you want. Make them in several sizes, and amaze your friends.

Closures

You'll see a wide variety of closures on the pieces in our book, from none (bangles or memory wire) to handmade, like those shown in action below.

The most important things to consider when choosing clasps are weight and points of attachment. Heavy clasps pull down to the bottom of your wrist, and that may or may not work for your design. Think of your clasp as one of the elements of (and a reflection on) your work. All points of connection should be gentle, with smooth metal edges and spacious rings. If you sew to metal rings, you might connect your work to them with bead-covered loops large enough to let their rings move freely.

Our favorite clasps are those that work with the beadwork, like hidden snaps, sewn not into the bead holes but into the network of thread connecting them. See Deb Bednarek's lovely tailoring on her Helix Bracelet (pg. 197) for an example of a combination of an inner snap and a button and loop.

Beaded toggles are lovely, but must be well-crafted to stand the extra wear. We love Tiena Habing's square toggle bar on her Ocular Chain (pg. 37).

Below, right: Beadwork by Kate McKinnon, clasps by Kate (fine silver, the *Lovely Bone*) and Stephanie Price (copper, the *Walker Clasp*). These clasps are removable, and slide into slender tubes sewn into the ends of the beadwork. See our companion eBook for a tutorial on making them, or our web site, www.ContemporaryGeometricBeadwork.com, for places to purchase them.

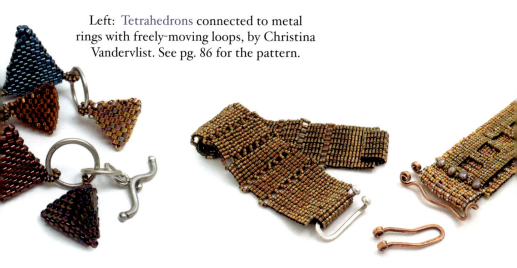

Left: Tetrahedrons connected to metal rings with freely-moving loops, by Christina Vandervlist. See pg. 86 for the pattern.

Basics: Simple Flat Square

This shape is the base of the Pyramid Bangle (pg. 84). The basic pattern was adapted by Cate Jones from those used previously by Julia Pretl and Diane Fitzgerald, and it stays nice and flat unless you work it too tightly. The actual size of 9 rounds, worked in 11° cylinder beads, is about 1/2" square.

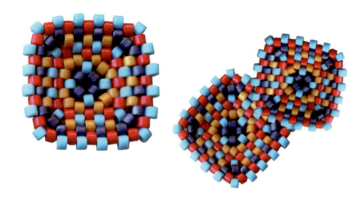

Round 1:   Join 4 beads into a circle, and pass through at least one to secure your thread.

Round 2:   Using circular peyote stitch, place 1 bead in each gap.

Round 3:   Add 3 beads in each space (the middle of these three is part of the "X" pattern you can see in the structure).

Round 4:   Add 2 beads over the top of the centre bead of the triplets placed in Round 3, and 1 bead in each side space.

Round 5:   Point Round: peyote 1 bead in each space, including 1 between each corner pair.

Round 6:   Fill Round: peyote 1 bead in each space.

Round 7:   Peyote 1 bead in each side space and 3 in the corners.

Round 8:   Peyote 1 bead in each side space as well as 2 beads in each corner, over the centre bead of the triplet.

Round 9:   Point Round: peyote 1 bead in each side space and 1 bead between each pair in the corners. Continue repeating the pattern until your Flat Square is the desired size.

Materials: medium weight beading thread (we used Nymo B)
               1 g. 11° cylinder beads

Technique: circular peyote

Tension: soft to moderate

Difficulty: You can do it!

Although the most visually exciting Squares are probably those made with block and line patterns, we think that it's easier to learn circular beading if every round is a different colour. This is especially true when the instructions seem improbable, as in this pattern, which tells you to put three beads on each corner, and then stack two beads on top of those. It sounds absurd, we know, but look how easy it is to see when drawn in alternate-colour rounds.

The style and size of bead that you use will drastically affect the look, feel and behavior of your Squares. Each of these takes only a few minutes to make, so it's a perfect project to explore size and finish combinations. See Francesca Walton's mixed-bead squares on pg. 33 for inspiration.

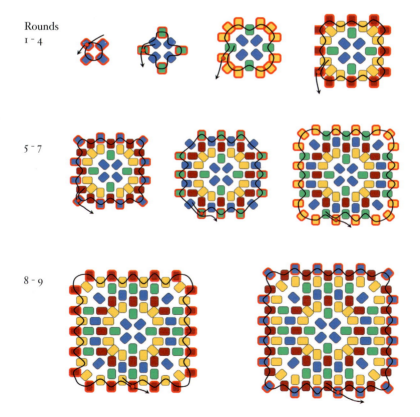

Rounds 1 - 4

5 - 7

8 - 9

Contemporary Geometric Beadwork by Kate McKinnon   29

Basics: Warped Square

This square will warp almost right away, and can be used to build fantastic shapes like Jean Power's *Geometric Stars*, and Phyllis Dintenfass's *Tetraphyls,* both shown on the opposite page. Bead this one tightly!

 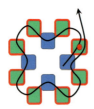 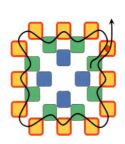 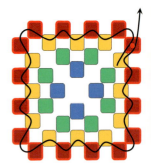

Round 1   Join 4 beads into a circle, and pass through the first bead strung to secure your thread.

Round 2:   Using circular peyote stitch, place two beads in each corner. These will form the herringbone rib increases of your Square.

Round 3
to end: Peyote a bead in each gap, and continue to add two beads at each corner. Repeat until the square is the desired size, and finish with a Point Round if desired.

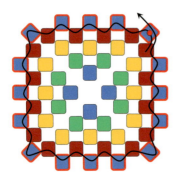

A Point Round is one bead in every space, transforming corners into points.

If you are making a form that you plan to begin decreasing, your Point Round will generally be followed by a Fill Round, in which you again add only one bead per space.

See Decreasing a Triangle into a Puff (pg. 58) for more on this.

Jean Power

Warped Squares can be used as pattern pieces to build other shapes. Jean Power zips five of them together to make her glorious Geometric Star puffs, above, by Jean, and right, by Dana Steen Witker. See Jean's pattern in her beautiful book, *Jean Power's Geometric Beadwork*, 2012.

Phyllis Dintenfass connected five Warped Squares end-to-end to make her *Tetraphyls* bracelet below, and strung 58 of them on cord for the elegantly graduated chain of colour on the following page.

Phyllis Dintenfass

Contemporary Geometric Beadwork by Kate McKinnon

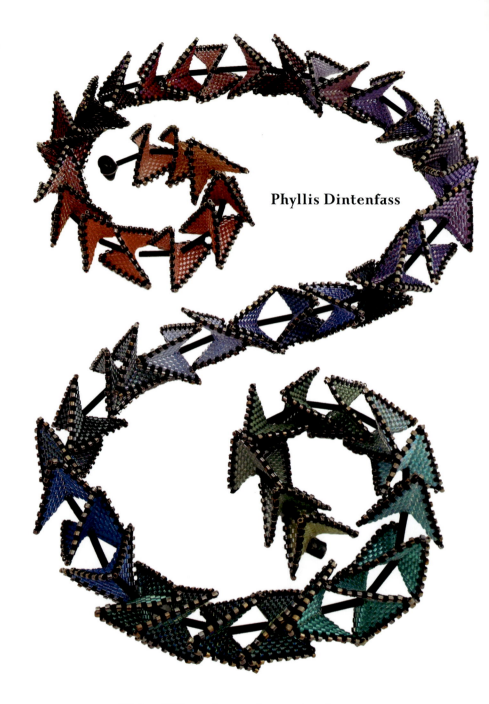

Phyllis Dintenfass

"Colour! What a deep and mysterious language, the language of dreams."

Paul Gauguin

Francesca Walton

Francesca uses different bead sizes and shapes in her patterns and makes several different kinds of squares. The little spaceships excited us hugely, and we all wanted to make her *Axe of the Warrior Goddess* earrings, above.

A view of the transition from outdoor to indoor space in John Lautner's astonishing Sheats-Goldstein house in Los Angeles. *Photo Woolf Haxton, www.thevhf.com*

Spending an evening inside this house rewired Kate's brain, and Lautner's influence can be seen in each soar of a Wing and every improbable extension of a Horn in this book.

The structure of the roof is a master study in positive and negative space, and it seems both to float and to be infinitely strong; at once massive and delicate, built of heavy concrete and glass. Lautner embedded heavy cocktail glasses in the concrete to let in the light and sparkle, as we might set crystals in a field of matte beads.

An interesting thing about this particular roof is that it is clearly capable of carrying more, like the Bands in our pieces. Restrained power is a design element in itself, and we see it in Rayo Boursier's *Horned Cuff* (right).

It takes discipline to have a powerful structure, and such potential, and yet not send the house or the cuff winging off in every direction.

34   Contemporary Geometric Beadwork by Kate McKinnon

Basics: MRAW Bellybands

Buckminster Fuller said, when explaining his beautiful geodesic frame structures to traditionalists, "To change something, make a new model that makes the existing models obsolete."

We don't think we rendered anything obsolete with our beautiful Band, but we definitely made some new things and thought some new thoughts by working this way, and by thinking architecturally. Our Wings and Horns, our Rick-Rack Bangles, our Fortunetellers, our Sea Monsters...our Tri-Wing Rings...all of these and more are built on our fabulous Bellyband.

Practice this little marvel to make sure that you've got the thread path correct (in this case, the Path is definitely the Power) and that you can make it snug and tight. Experiment with the things we bypassed with this Band, and then see what you can make or alter by adding our little powerhouse element.

Below, in her Horned Cuff, Rayo chose to repeat the Band throughout her piece as a decorative element. This plays beautifully off of the concept of the structure, and also, like Lautner's leaded crystal circles in the concrete roof, the windows left by her Bands bring light to her piece, and allow the beads that appear from the outside to be metallic flat beige to glow like sunshine from the inside.

What more could we ask from enclosing space?

Opposite page: two Tri-Wing Rings by Kate McKinnon echo both Lautner's elegant roof and Fuller's geodesic dome sections.

Right: a Horned Cuff by Rayo Boursier. See this piece also on pg. 94.

"Ideas rose in clouds; I felt them collide until pairs interlocked, making a stable combination."

Henri Poincaré

Contemporary Geometric Beadwork by Kate McKinnon   35

Basics: MRAW (Modified Right Angle Weave) Bellybands

The Bellyband (sometimes referred to simply as "The Band") offers many opportunities to build more structure from the starting point, as the RAW will easily accept more rows of work, or support Guide Rounds, Helix Points, or whatever you want to build on it. Not only did the Band lead us to Wings and Horns, but it revealed itself as being a useful start for Geometric Rope like the Power Puff Bangle, offering an easy zip with no unbeading required.

We want to be clear that "MRAW" is a thread path, not a different stitch. The "M" for "Modified" refers only to the build of the Band- instead of making a RAW band and going back into the work to place the first round of peyote, our lovely thread path moves in only one direction (instead of the back and forth looping of regular RAW) and places the first round of peyote in the first pass of beadwork.

So, as you will see, the "MRAW" refers to the creation of the band, but after that, in the beadwork, the Band is just a run of ordinary RAW, and the spacer round becomes simply the first round of peyote.

Above: some neat *Sixagons* by Cath Thomas, built on an inner-band MRAW start and a peyote outer closure, photo by Cath. She enjoyed the MRAW start and was pleased to see that pieces like her Jalisco Bangle (pg. 214) could be made more quickly and with more options with a Band than with a peyote start. She was particularly interested in the concept of the Removable Band, which you can see in action on the TinyHorn Bangle, pg. 114.

Above: a round of MRAW replaces the Point Round in a Power Puff Rope by Eileen Montgomery.

Below: Tiena Habing's stunning *Ocular Chain*. Each element begins with a quick inner band MRAW start, and is finished on the outer edge with another MRAW Band in a bright colour. Tiena connected her elements and made her toggle bar with 3-D or Cubic RAW, which uses RAW for the sides, top and the bottom of a form. Once you start playing with Right Angle Weave, you will find it to be very architectural, useful for building or beginning almost any shape or form.

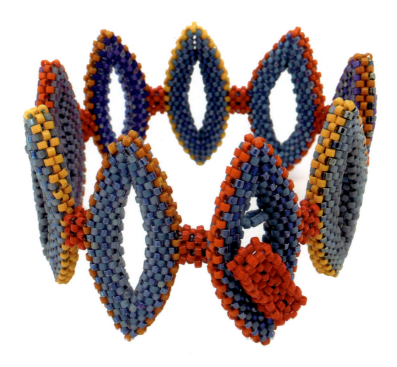

Basics: MRAW Bellybands

RAW (Right Angle Weave) Bellyband

To fully appreciate our nifty MRAW Bellyband, you need to make a regular RAW band first, changing directions with each unit added, and then go back into it to add a first peyote round. It makes us tired just thinking about it. You can make this band flat (for a strap bracelet, for example) or join it into a circle (for a bangle).

RAW uses 4-bead units. The first one is added in a group of four, the rest in groups of three. To join the band into a circle, you will use two beads. We used cylinder beads for our examples, but you can combine beads in these bands with great effect.

Step 1: Pick up four beads, join them into a circle, and pass back through the first two added to secure the thread and prepare for the next add.

Step 2: Pick up three beads, and pass down through the bead that you came down through to begin the unit. Pass through the bottom bead and the right hand bead to complete the unit and prepare for the next add.

Step 3: Pick up three beads, and pass up through the bead that you came up through to begin the unit. See how you are changing directions with each unit added?

Step 4: Repeat Step 2 and Step 3 to continue the band to the desired length.

Step 5: Join the band into a circle (optional). To do this, pick up one bead, pass through the first bead of the first unit, pick up another bead, and then pass through the last bead of the last unit. Reinforce the join by passing through more beads.

Step 6: Add one bead into each space in one of the two Toothrows of RAW to add a first peyote row or round.

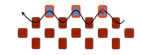

MRAW (Modified Right Angle Weave) Bellyband

Our elegant MRAW Bellyband is a quicker path to the goal, with no change of direction. In one pass of beadwork, you get a full RAW band and a spacer row, which ends up to be your first round of peyote.

We strongly recommend using a different colour for your spacers, so that you can see the structure. Pay attention to the thread path; it matters! You should only pass through the spacer beads once, when you pick them up with your needle. To complete the unit, bypass the spacer bead and pass directly through the top bead of the unit. (See Step 2, below.)

Bypass the spacer bead in the same way each time for a smooth band. We like to pass in front of the spacer bead, rather than behind it.

Step 1: Pick up four beads, join them into a circle, and pass back through the first bead.

Step 2: Pick up a spacer bead and three RAW beads, and, *bypassing the spacer bead,* pass through the top RAW bead. You are in position for the next add. Repeat until your Band is the desired length. Each stitch will be the same.

Step 3: Join the Band into a circle (optional). Be sure to go through enough beads after closure to neatly secure the join (see detail below). You are now at the same point as you were at the RAW band after two rounds. Whee!

Step 4: Step up and continue your piece as desired.

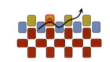

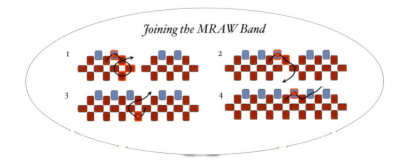

Joining the MRAW Band

Contemporary Geometric Beadwork by Kate McKinnon   39

Basics: MRAW Bellybands

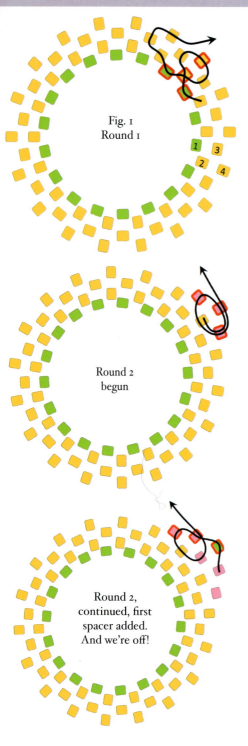

Fig. 1
Round 1

Round 2 begun

Round 2, continued, first spacer added. And we're off!

Double MRAW Bands

Sometimes a design will call for more architecture, or more layers, and you will want to make a double or triple MRAW Bellyband for a base or central element.

Even a single MRAW Band offers many options. In Fig. 1 (left) we numbered four potential rounds of beadwork to build on, two of which (the edges, 1 and 4) are Toothrounds. A double Band (Fig. 2, opposite page, top) will give you seven rounds.

Please note that these numbers, 1-4, or 1-7, don't relate to the construction of the Band, which is (fabulously) only one round of beadwork. We numbered them only to show you where your options and I-Beams are. As rounds can be built on both sides, even a single Bellyband gives you a sturdy base for eight potential layers of work.

Christina Vandervlist's *Triple Crown Rick-Rack* (opposite page, bottom) was built on a double MRAW Zigged Band (see next pages). She used three of the potential seven base rounds to make it.

The Helix Bangle (pgs. 196-209) uses a double Band to hold its six rounds of Points. Build your Bands strong and tight, and join them securely!

Remember, the band isn't really flat. We just drew it that way to show it better, It's a ring, and the added layers grow out to the sides or the top of it. In the Triple Crown Rick-Rack at right, the band is sitting contentedly at the bottom of the piece.

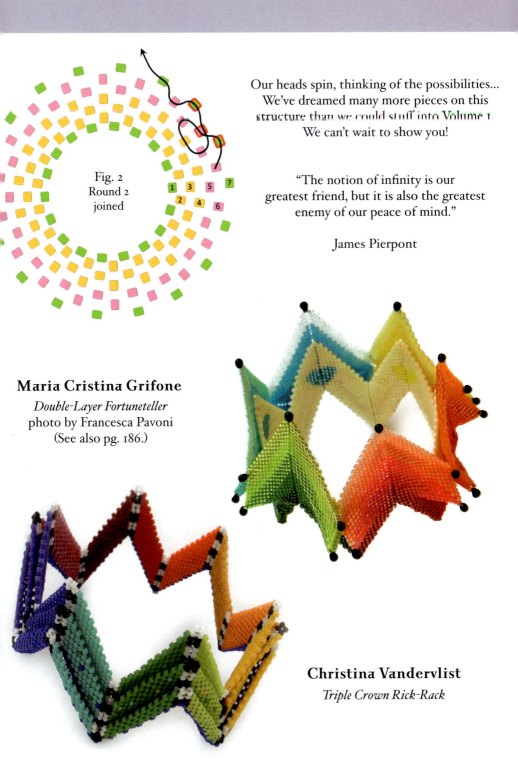

Fig. 2
Round 2
joined

Our heads spin, thinking of the possibilities...
We've dreamed many more pieces on this
structure than we could stuff into Volume 1.
We can't wait to show you!

"The notion of infinity is our
greatest friend, but it is also the greatest
enemy of our peace of mind."

James Pierpont

Maria Cristina Grifone
Double-Layer Fortuneteller
photo by Francesca Pavoni
(See also pg. 186.)

Christina Vandervlist
Triple Crown Rick-Rack

Contemporary Geometric Beadwork by Kate McKinnon

Basics: MRAW Bellybands

Zigged MRAW Bellyband

Our Zigged Band takes the fabulous up a notch by giving you a Rick-Rack structure in only one pass of beadwork. (Really, a single trumpet should blow on a hilltop whenever anyone reads that line. It's that exciting to us!) We do this by using our integral spacers (the "M" part of the MRAW) to add the increases and decreases that form the classic zig-zag pattern.

Of course, you can always add increases and/or decreases later, or at any point, but this start is a fabulous way to get immediate and architectural results, and allows you to avoid the only alternative zig-zag start we know, a foot-long worm of peyote.

Use a separate colour for the spacer round, so it's easy to see what you are making. We used cylinder beads for all of our MRAW Band examples, but you can also use seed beads or combine bead types for elegant results. You can leave the RAW grid showing in your work, as we do, or fill the gaps with crystals or other embellishment. We like to see the structure, it thrills us. Follow your star.

See the TinyHorn Bangle, pg. 114, to make a Removable Bellyband.

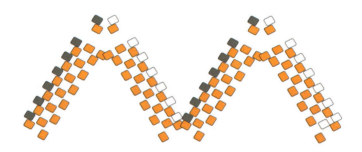

To make a Zigged Band, begin a regular MRAW Band (see pg. 39) but instead of a spacer round of single beads, place increases and decreases in regular increments around the Band.

Our example places them in every seventh spacer-space, and is the pattern we used to make the Bands and the Rick-Rack on the opposite page. Please see the Rick-Rack section, pgs. 136-155, and the Fortuneteller Bangle, pgs. 164-195, for more ways to build on this excellent Zigged Band.

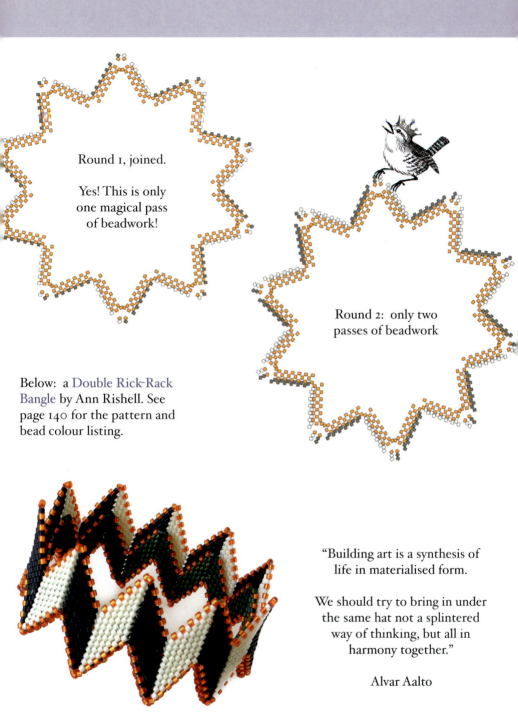

Round 1, joined.

Yes! This is only one magical pass of beadwork!

Round 2: only two passes of beadwork

Below: a Double Rick-Rack Bangle by Ann Rishell. See page 140 for the pattern and bead colour listing.

"Building art is a synthesis of life in materialised form.

We should try to bring in under the same hat not a splintered way of thinking, but all in harmony together."

Alvar Aalto

Left: Triangle Earrings by Christina Vandervlist. These lovelies are just little Flat Peyote Triangles (pattern on pg. 50) sewn to lengths of six-bead peyote tube. It's just as easy to imagine them hung on bits of chain, wire, or beading cable.

Below: Power Puff Bangle by Suzanne Golden.

Opposite, top: Power Puff Bangle in 15° cylinder beads by Lia Melia

Opposite, bottom: Flat Peyote Triangles by Kate McKinnon

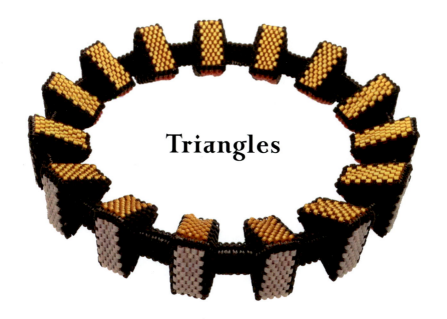

Triangles

"The triangle is the only structure.
It holds the universe together."

Buckminster Fuller

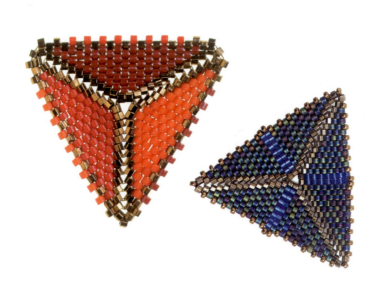

Flat Peyote Triangle

The clean fabric of peyote stitch is perfect for making geometric shapes, and the addition of herringbone-style increases makes corners, wings and folds, which allow you to build forms. Three of these increases placed in flat circular peyote make a spoked triangle.

These simple, elegant shapes are fun to make, and are great little canvases for swatching colours or testing patterns or bead finishes.

They make beautiful jewelry, and they are also the beginning of the Power Puff and Caldera Bangles, which you are surely going to want to make as well. How could you not?

Above: Wired-loop Triangle Bracelet by Jodie Marshall
Opposite page: Triangles by Kate McKinnon and Dustin Wedekind

Flat Peyote Triangle

The lovely peyote triangle can be made in any size or combination of beads. We prefer cylinder beads for clean and straight geometric work, but frequently use rounds for edging or for the center rings. If you use only 11° round beads to make this pattern, it will be wavy.

Different bead finishes will show their personalities in this structure, and the amount of tension and kind of thread used will determine the stiffness or softness of the finished piece. Even within the same bead size, variations in tailoring will show. Some beads or bead combinations will make cupped triangles, some flat.

If you are just learning, make a handful, and combine a variety of colours, patterns, and finishes. You'll rapidly see how even small things like a matte surface or a shiny or coated finish can change the way the beadwork behaves, and you'll get some good practice with step-ups, error-free increases, and keeping your work smooth and tight.

Triangles on both pages by Kate McKinnon and Dustin Wedekind
Above: Photo of Gabriella van Diepen by Kyle Cassidy

We promise that it's worth the time to get this right, and feel comfortable Triangling before moving on to more complex forms, so that key maneuvers like stepping up and controlling the thread become second nature. Because as soon as you can control the beads and the thread, you can make anything!

"Expression and shape are almost more to me than knowledge itself. My work has always tried to unite the true with the beautiful, and when I have had to choose one or the other, I usually chose the beautiful."

Hermann Weyl

Flat Peyote Triangle

Materials: medium weight beading thread (Nymo B or equivalent)
2 g. 11° cylinder beads

Technique: circular peyote, herringbone
Tension: moderate to snug, as desired

Difficulty: You can do it!

We used 11° Miyuki Delicas:
(A)   254   Bronze Hex
(B)   659   Capri Blue
(C)   798   Dark Capri Blue
(D)   651   Yellow

This simple little pattern is one of the three keys to our universe; if you can make a Flat Peyote Triangle, a Power Puff Ring and a Tri-Wing Ring, you can make anything in this book.

In light of that, give the Triangle your full attention, make it tight, make it dance. (But most of all, make more than one. See pg. 44 for a great pair of earrings to entice you to go wild practicing these.)

Watch For Hidden Step Ups!

To help recognize the magical moment when you've completed a row or a round and are ready to step up to begin the next one, use a different colour or tone (like our blues) for each round.

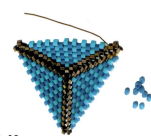

Another way to flag the completion of a side, a row or a round is to set out the beads needed before you begin it (see photo at right).

See more on stepping up in circular peyote in Basics, pg. 25.

50   Contemporary Geometric Beadwork by Kate McKinnon

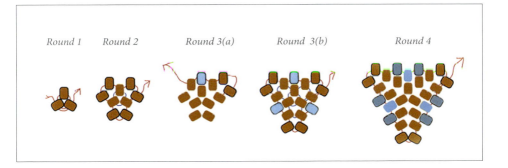

Round 1:   Pick up 3 (A) beads, and join them into a circle. Pass through the first bead again to secure the thread.

Round 2:   Using circular peyote stitch, add 2 (A) beads in each space. Pass your needle through the first bead of the previous round to "step up" and end the round. Your completed Round 2 will form the base of each of the three herringbone ribs, which the peyote stitch will climb.

Rounds 3 & 4:   Add 2 (A) beads to each rib, and peyote stitch 1 (B) bead into each side space on Round 3. Step up at the end of the round.

Repeat for Round 4, using (C) beads for the side spaces. You will be adding one more bead on each side of each round of increase, as you can see by comparing the diagrams for 3b and 4. (Round 3 has one blue bead per side, while Round 4 has two.)

Rounds 5 & up: Continue adding rounds, alternating (B) and (C) beads (or following your own pattern, of course) until your triangle is the desired size. We did 12 rounds, finishing with a round of bright yellow (D) beads.

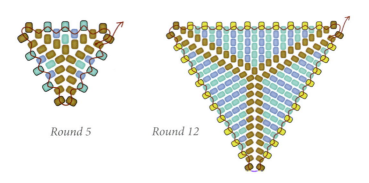

Flat Peyote Triangle: The Six Bead Start

If you'd like triangles with bigger holes in the center, perhaps for making earrings, wired jewelry, or to place them on metal posts, start with six beads instead of three.

Round 1:   Pick up 6(A) beads. Join the beads into a circle, and pass through all six beads again to reinforce the hole and secure the thread.

Round 2:   Add 2(A) beads in the gaps between each pair of beads. These adds form the base of each of the three herringbone ribs, just as in the traditional Three-Bead Start.

Round 3:   Add 2(A) beads to each rib, and choose to place either 1 or 2(B) beads in each center side space on Round 3. For a racing stripe two beads wide, place two beads.

Proceed as usual, placing either one or two beads in the center spaces, depending on the choice you made in Round 3.

Rounds 1-5

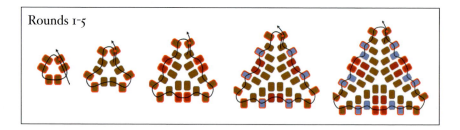

This start can be deployed to make either a swank racing stripe (with two beads in the center side spaces, as above) or with a regular peyote side fill that places a single bead (left). As you might imagine, a Six-Bead Start with a one-bead fill will make a slightly cupped, spinny shape.

Above: a Six-Bead Start on a Power Puff by Dustin Wedekind, with a sporty two-bead racing stripe in hot red.

Above right: the same start, by Kate, with a one-bead beginning to the peyote fill. The one-bead fill makes the red triangle cup in at the center.

Below: holes in these triangles allow them to be easily set on wires or posts, as Jodie Marshall did in this bracelet. See another view of this piece on page 47.

Contemporary Geometric Beadwork by Kate McKinnon

Adding A Point Round

The addition of a Point Round makes for a neat finish, and also makes a nice transition into a decrease, turning your flat triangle into a three-dimensional Power Puff.

In a Point Round, only one bead is placed in each corner space. These single beads form the "points" at the triangle tips, and make a nice finish round for a flat triangle if you use 11° or 15° rounds, or other smooth beads.

Below, Fig. 1 shows where we stopped increasing our triangle in Round 12.

Fig. 2 shows the addition of Round 13, a Point Round. Kate used small round 15° beads for the corners. Cylinder beads, drops, crystals, or 11° rounds work in the Point Rounds as well, and each has a different effect.

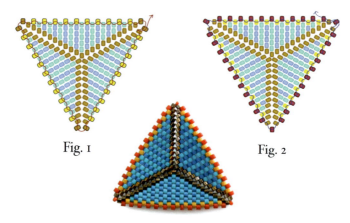

Fig. 1   Fig. 2

Fig. 2, photo

Whether it is used to add depth, to begin a tube, or to begin a decrease, the next round only fills the spaces. It's rather a distinctive round, though, and we thought it should have a name, so we called it a Fill Round.

If you continue adding alternating Point and Fill Rounds with no increase or decrease, the beadwork forms a tube. This is a good way to add depth to the Puffs.

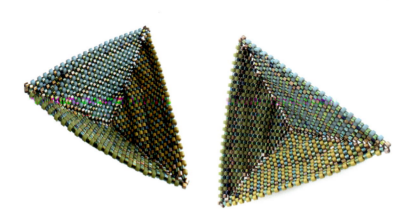

Above: multiple Point Rounds can be added to a piece to provide depth. Dustin took advantage of stepped increases to form a geometric bowl. To do this, after every four rounds of increase, he added a Point and then a Fill Round. See Tetrahedrons, pg. 86, for more stepped fun.

Below: Point Rounds can be done entirely in sparklies as well, as A.J. Reardon did to great effect when she used 2mm olivine Swarovski crystals for each Point Round in her Power Puff Bangle.

Turning Triangles Into Puffs

Decreasing a Flat Peyote Triangle into a Puff is an exciting move that begins a dimensional, geometric exploration of the form.

In the following pages, we'll show Power Puff Rings, Power Puff and Caldera Bangles, earrings, MRAW Bellyband starts, Pyramid Bangles, and other delights built on the noble triangle. Soak in the possibilities...

Above: three exquisite Power Puff Bangles by Jean Power. We only wish you could play with them!

Above: a Caldera Bangle by Maria Cristina Grifone, with Puffs forming a twirling cascade of form and colour. *Photo by Francesca Pavoni.*

Below: three swatches by (left to right) Jean Power, Dustin Wedekind and Kate McKinnon. Lengths like this can become bangles, Geometric Rope, stunning earrings, or can simply be kept as samples for reference.

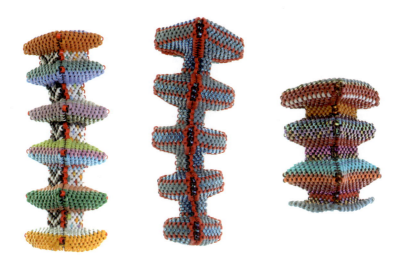

Decreasing Into A Puff

 Pearl Of Wisdom

The Puff rib decrease is created in a different way than the increase; instead of adding pairs (as you do in an increase) the rib decrease is *pulled* together, and no beads are added. It's really fascinating that the finished structure of the back side of a Puff is identical to that of the front, considering how differently they go together. Normally a thread path will define a shape, but in this case, the results are the same front and back.

To understand how geometric peyote grows, makes tubes, and decreases, you only need to remember three things:

> Add **2** beads at the corners to make an increase
> Add **1** bead at the corners to hold (as in a Point Round)
> Add **0** beads at the corners to decrease

When increasing the triangle, two rib beads are added at each corner, but in the decrease, the ribs develop (both structurally and visually) as you pass through the last and first beads of each side of the previous round.

This is hugely important when working a pattern, to remember that you really *are* adding corners to each round. You are simply doing it in advance. The first and last beads of each side actually belong to the round yet to come; they are building blocks for the future.

In Fig. 2 (opposite) note the bronze beads added at the ends of each side of the Fill Round. You'll see them become rib beads in the very next round.

When Christina teaches this decrease, she refers to these future rib beads as "shoulder" beads. She tells her students, "When you get to the shoulders, pass through both of them to draw them into hunchbacks."

After adding a Point Round to the Flat Peyote Triangle, you can add one Fill Round (see Basics, pg. 24), and then the first round of your decrease. If you wish, alternate a few Point and Fill Rounds before you begin decreasing to deepen the Puff.

Fig. 1

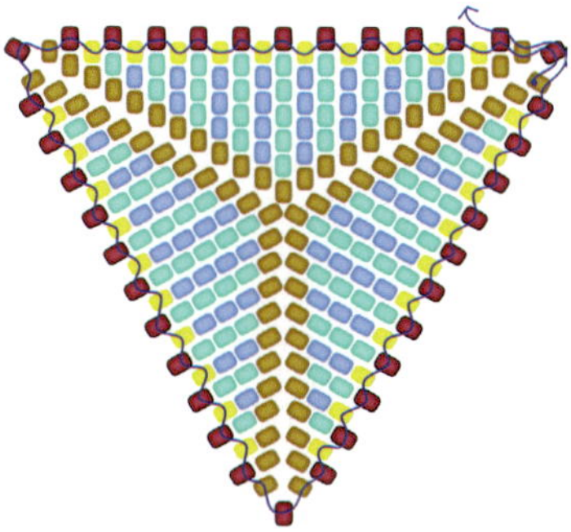

Fig. 1

Flat Peyote Triangle with Point Round added.

Fig. 2

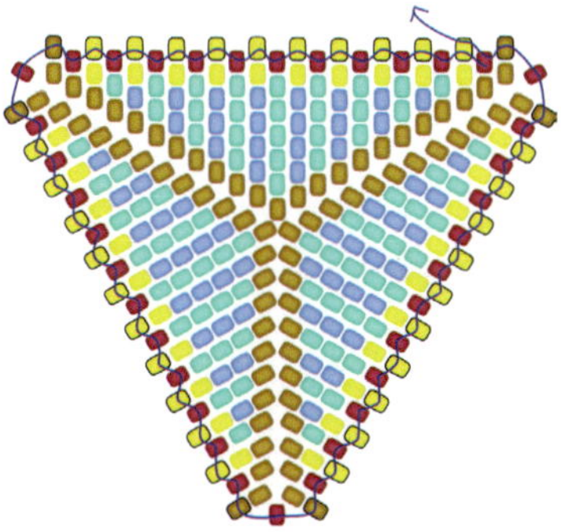

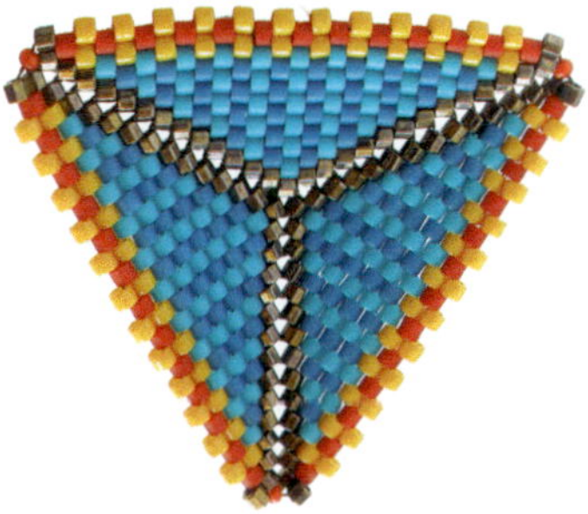

Fig. 2: Fill Round

Add 12 beads to each side for the first round of the decrease. We wanted the visual effect of the bronze hex ribs to continue, so we added 1(A), 10(D), 1(A).

The beads in this round are identically placed to those in the last round of the increase. You can see this when you compare Figs. 1 and 2.

Fig. 2, photo

Pass through each of the Point Round beads to add the Fill Round, which is the first round of the decreasing Puff. It will seem as if the new round is extending outward, but it will pull inward in the very next round.

Contemporary Geometric Beadwork by Kate McKinnon 59

Decreasing Into A Puff

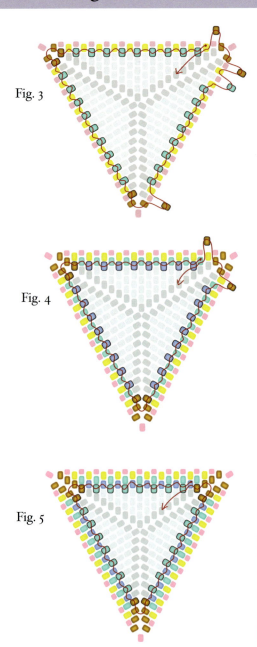

Fig. 3

Fig. 4

Fig. 5

Fig. 3: **First Round of Decrease**

Add 11 beads to each side. We used 1(A), 9(D), and 1(A). Bypass the Point beads in the corners, and pass through the two shoulder beads on either side, drawing them together.

Fig. 4: two more future rib beads have been added at the ends of each side, and the two previous end beads on each side have been pulled into ribs.

Fig. 5: this illustration shows the third round of decrease at the same point in the piece.

Continue decreasing by one bead per round, passing through the corner beads, until the Puff is closed to the desired diameter.

> Would you like to make a Power Puff Ring?
>
> A Caldera or Power Puff Bangle?
>
> A pair of earrings?
>
> We've got you covered! Turn the pages to see the options.

Left: we are halfway through the stitch in Fig. 3. The next step is to bypass the Point bead, pass through the bronze hex bead, and only then do you add the first bead of the next side (which will be a bronze hex, of course, as it will be a rib bead in the next round).

Right: Puffs in the middle of a decrease. Each of these Puffs is at a good point to begin a tube connection to another Puff in a Geometric Rope or Power Puff Bangle.

Make your connecting tube any length or diameter you'd like, and remember that you can vary each element from Puff to Puff.

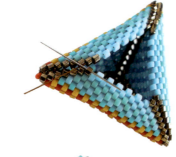

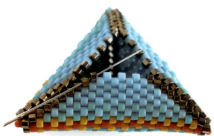

Left: a swatch by Kate, featuring Puffs of differing sizes. Making a necklace-length Geometric Rope is a great way to develop skill and to experiment with different Puff and tube sizes, Point Round treatments and styles.

Power Puff Ring and Bezel

Left: two Power Puff Rings by Dustin Wedekind.

Dustin used super-precise 11° Toho Aiko beads for these beauties.

A Power Puff Ring can be closed all or part of the way on the decrease. For a solid Puff, like those above, continue decreasing until you reach the center and weave in the thread. Turn to page 64 for a peyote shank pattern, and instructions on how to attach it. Alternatively, use the open section to bezel a stone or bead, or to build a ring shank or other form.

The Puffs make lovely pendants too. On the opposite page, lower left, you can see how Marcia DeCoster used a Puff to bezel a Swarovski crystal triangle. She placed the crystal inside the Puff, fixed it in place by decreasing the opening of the Puff to contain it (if the stone has a hole, sew through that as well) and then she embellished the bezel for extra sparkle. A simple strap attached to the top forms an easy yet elegant pendant bail.

Below, and as in the earrings on page 44, Christina Vandervlist grew Puffs from slender six-bead even count peyote tubes to make irresistible elements.

Above: a Power Puff Bangle in progress by Kate McKinnon, sporting hot red point beads and a Racing Stripe that fades in and out.

To make a Racing Stripe, see the Six-Bead Start, pg. 52).

Above: Helen Fountain

Left: Marcia DeCoster

Marcia and Helen each used Puffs as bezels. Marcia used Swarovski's Fancy Stone #4370 in her pendant.

Contemporary Geometric Beadwork by Kate McKinnon   63

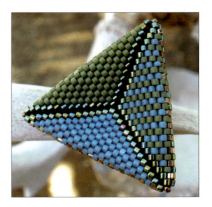

Sew the finished shank to the Puff like a button. Either sew both layers together as below, or sew the shank only to the bottom layer before closing the Puff. Rings on this page by Dustin Wedekind.

64 Contemporary Geometric Beadwork by Kate McKinnon

Power Puff Ring Shank

Materials:	medium weight beading thread (we used Nymo B) 5 g. of seed or cylinder beads (we used 11° Miyuki Delica cylinders and 1 g. of 15° Miyuki rounds)
Technique:	flat peyote with optional square stitch edging
Tension:	snug
Difficulty:	You can do it!

We love this shank made as a separate attachment, but if you prefer to build yours directly off of your Puff, it's easy to do (see Dustin's orange example on the opposite page). For rings that can take a lot of wear, though, we recommend a two piece solution.

To make our shank, begin with an arm's length of medium to heavy thread (we use Nymo B or D), pick up five beads, and follow these simple diagrams. Build your shank long enough for a custom fit.

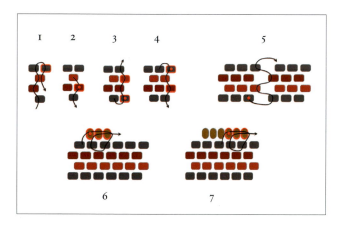

Assuming the tension used to make the band is sensibly snug, it won't shrink much when it's closed and finished. The 15° rounds at the edge can be used for a bit of light tailoring, by taking a reinforcing pass through them and pulling them a bit tighter. Doing this doesn't change the size of the band, but it brings the edges in for a closer fit, and makes the shank sturdier.

Power Puff & Caldera Bangles

Opposite: Power Puff and Caldera Bangles by
Jean Power and Kate McKinnon

Above: Power Puff Bangle in greens by Leslie Venturoso

Left: photo of Gabriella van Diepen by Kyle Cassidy

"Architecture starts when you
carefully put two bricks together.
There it begins."

Mies van der Rohe

Power Puff Bangle

The Power Puff Bangle is one of many spectacular Geometric Rope designs from Jean Power, and its simple genius engaged our minds from the first. Seeing the bangle is one thing. Holding it is entirely another. The way it moves, and how it looks as you roll it through its paces, how it contracts and expands, how many faces present themselves for attention or design detail... to hold a Power Puff is to love it.

Although it is a complex form visually, this bangle is simple to grasp. If you've made a Power Puff Ring, you already have the *mad skilz* required. And the Power Puff and the Caldera Bangle are essentially the same structure; the Puff just has a bit more tube (consecutive Point and Fill Rounds) between elements.

Once you make a Caldera or a Power Puff Bangle, you'll know all you need to know about making Geometric Rope. Triangles, pentagons, squares, balls... any shape you learn or dream up can be built on the architecture of circular peyote, using herringbone increases, point rounds, and peyote decreases.

The bangle below was beaded by Kate, using leftover or odd lot 11° cylinder beads. Hot red 13° Czech rounds at the tip of each Puff and tube section give a nice pointy pop and lend your eye a steady path through the colours.

Kim Boeckman
Confetti Power Puff

Kim used 11° Miyuki Delicas in matte black (DB310) and a confetti mix of leftover beads from other projects.

Helen Fountain
Power Puff Earrings

Helen used 8° Toho rounds in #2012 and 11° Miyuki Delicas to make these nifty Puff Earrings:

375
389
653

Soldered rings could easily be substituted for the beaded loops attaching the Puff Segments to the earwires, adding both longevity and a more traditional gallery appeal.

Caldera Bangle

The Caldera is another splendid Jean Power pattern. It's a Power Puff Bangle with no tube between Puffs, worked in a vibrant pattern. It uses a main colour as a stripe, leaving small sections to fill with one or many additional colours. For this bangle, Jean chose black for her stripe, and then went wild in her bead stash and used over 70 different colours to fill in. This is the perfect piece to use small quantities of beads left over from other projects.

Take a minute to study how it goes together, and think about how to section it, how different it would look with just one or two colours, with a rainbow fade, in black and white...the design possibilities of patterns like this are limitless, and they fascinate us.

The Caldera bangles, with no tube between Puffs, look quite different from ropier Power Puff versions. This rapid transition from Puff to Puff is a good way to make a very tight pattern, with style elements easily flowing from one Puff to the next.

Amusingly, in edit, Doriot Lair said that these bangles look like flags at the United Nations. They do!

Kirsty Little
Lairy Caldera

Beads used:
11° Miyuki Delicas:

10	727
659	751
661	763
722	

Christina Porter
Beads used:
11° Miyuki Delicas:

29
63
651
862
864

Caldera Bangle

Planning your start:

If the Caldera is made as a clasped bracelet or on memory wire instead of as a bangle, only about 40 grams are needed. See Finishing Geometric Rope Bangles, pg. 79, to review your options before you begin beading.

Beads used: 11° Miyuki Delicas:

(A) Bead: DB 10, black, 8 g and (in numerical order) the rest:

60	691
76	692
88x	707
135	725
149	730
174	733
177	746
190	748
210	754
216	759
239	760
263	783
264	786
265	792
277	798
285	799
361	878
371	1052
373	1054
374	1209
375	1250
376	1284
378	1304
432	1341
627	1363
654	1376
658	1536
659	1566
660	1578
661	1769
685	1850

Above: Jean Power's original Caldera Bangle.

Below: Carla Engelman used a magnetic clasp for her Caldera, neatly sewn into the tube.

Materials: medium weight beading thread (we used Nymo B)
40-50 g. of 11° cylinder beads

Technique: circular peyote, herringbone

Tension: snug

Difficulty: Intermediate: start with the Flat Peyote Triangle and the Power Puff Ring

We know that we don't have to tell *you* how to make a Flat Peyote Triangle. Why, you probably made a bowlful of them half a chapter ago.

We included every step in this pattern because the Caldera is as much a pattern as it is a form. Also, if you are a new beader, it's easier to see it go together round by round. Later on in the book, when you are all fully seasoned Trianglers, we'll just toss a few salient facts at you and you'll whip out a bangle. Just like that.

Step 1   Begin a Flat Peyote Triangle with 3(A) beads. Leave a bit of tail to hang onto (it helps control tension).

Step 2   Using circular peyote stitch, add 2(B) beads in each space.

Step 3   Peyote stitch using 2(B) and 1(A). Repeat twice to finish the round.

Step 4   Peyote stitch using 2(B), 1(A) and 1(A). Repeat twice to finish the round.

Contemporary Geometric Beadwork by Kate McKinnon   73

Caldera Bangle

Peyote stitch using 2(B), 1(A), 1(C) and 1(A). Repeat twice to finish the round.

Step 5

Peyote stitch using 2(B), 1(A), 2(C) and 1(A). Repeat twice to finish the round.

Step 6

Peyote stitch using 2(B), 1(A), 3(C) and 1(A). Repeat twice to finish the round.

Step 7

Peyote stitch using 2(B), 1(A), 4(C) and 1(A). Repeat twice to finish the round.

Step 8

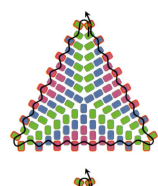

Peyote stitch using 2(B), 1(A), 2(C), 1(A), 2(C) and 1(A). Repeat twice to finish the round.

Step 9

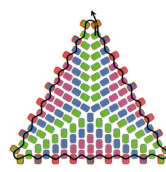

74   Contemporary Geometric Beadwork by Kate McKinnon

Step 10   Peyote stitch using 2(B), 1(A), 2(C), 2(A), 2(C) and 1(A). Repeat twice to finish the round.

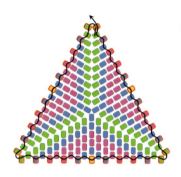

Step 11   Peyote stitch using 2(B), 1(A), 2(C), 1(A), 1(D), 1(A), 2(C) and 1(A). Repeat twice to finish the round. This is the last round of increase.

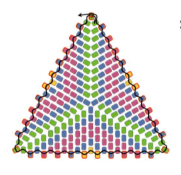

Step 12   **Point Round**
Peyote stitch using 1(B), 1(A), 2(C), 1(A), 2(D), 1(A), 2(C) and 1(A). Repeat twice to finish the round.

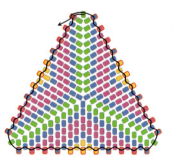

Step 13   **Fill Round**
Peyote stitch using 1(A), 2(C), 1(A), 3(D), 1(A), 2(C) and 1(A). Repeat twice to finish the round. Don't forget to step up at the end of your Fill Round and your Decrease Rounds, just as you do while increasing.

Caldera Bangle

The diagrams show completed previous rounds (which are now officially on the opposite side of the piece) in shadow, to make it easier to see how the new rounds being added relate to the other half of the form.

First Round of Decrease
Peyote stitch using 2(C), 1(A), 4(D), 1(A), 2(C) and no beads in the corner space. Instead, pass your needle through the existing corner beads to bring the sides together. Repeat twice to finish the round.

Step 14

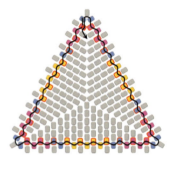

Peyote stitch using 1(C), 1(A), 2(D), 1(A), 2(D), 1(A), 1(C) and no beads in the corner space. Repeat twice to finish the round.

Step 15

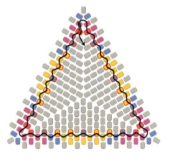

Peyote stitch using 1(A), 2(D), 2(A), 2(D), 1(A) and no beads in the corner space. Repeat twice to finish the round.

Step 16

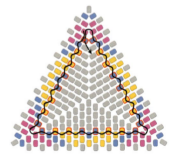

Contemporary Geometric Beadwork by Kate McKinnon

For a seamless colour match when the Caldera Bangle is connected, the (E) bead in the final half-Puff must be the same colour as the (B) bead used in the first half-Puff.

The beadwork should be behaving like a Puff now. If not, increase your tension, and keep your thread taut while you are working.

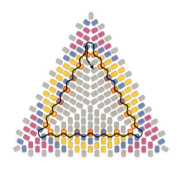

Step 17 — Peyote stitch using 2(D), 1(A), 1(E), 1(A), 2(D) and no beads in the corner space. Repeat twice to finish the round.

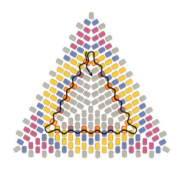

Step 18 — Peyote stitch using 1(D), 1(A), 2(E), 1(A), 1(D) and no beads in the corner space. Repeat twice to finish the round.

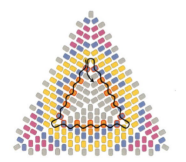

Step 19 — Peyote stitch using 1(A), 3(E), 1(A) and no beads in the corner space. Repeat twice to finish the round.

Caldera Bangle

Peyote stitch using 4(E) and no beads in the corner space. Repeat twice to finish the round.

Step 20

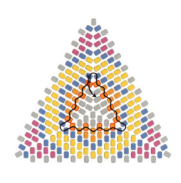

Peyote stitch using 1(E), 1(A), 1(E), and no beads in the corner space. Repeat twice to finish the round. You are now ready to increase again.

Step 21

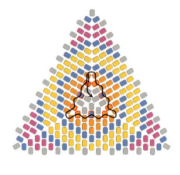

Needle forward to come out of the second (E) bead in this round. This way, the starting position on the next Puff will match the start on the first one, so the steps can be exactly repeated.

Step 22 (optional)

Repeat from Step 5, but use (E) beads instead of (B) as you increase the next Puff. Add in new colours from this point or repeat previous colours as you like. Continue creating Puffs until your Caldera is the desired length.

Step 23

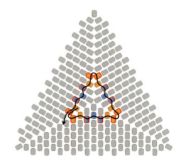

Finishing Geometric Rope Bangles

To make a clasped bracelet, attach the clasp at the most sensible points. A magnetic closure works beautifully inside a rope (see pgs. 72 and 226).

Memory wire: If you prefer not to use a clasp, but still want a close fit, cut a piece of medium to heavy memory wire, and slip it into the open tube of the beadwork. If the wire is sturdy enough, no overlap is necessary.

Joining the piece as a bangle. We have two good options for this:

1. Unbeading: Unbead the first triangle back to its Point Round (Step 12). Bead the other end of the work up to Step 11, and zip the two halves together to form the final Puff.

2. No Unbeading: Start the bangle at the tube connection, instead of in the center of a triangle. Make an MRAW Bellyband (pg. 39) in the diameter of the connecting tube. The Caldera has only one round of connection, so make a start to mimic Step 4, and begin following the pattern at Step 5.

Bead until the first Point Round. Stop work on that end, return to the start, and bead the bangle in the other direction. When ready to join, bead another Puff up to Step 11, then zip it to the Point Round of the beginning half-Puff.

See the photos below, swatch by Deb Bednarek.

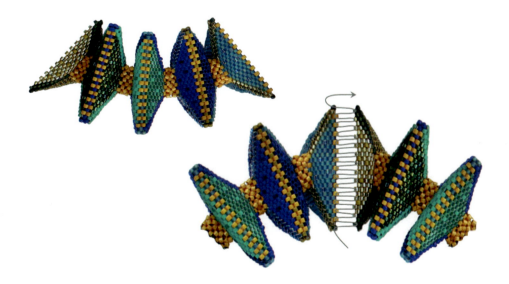

Contemporary Geometric Beadwork by Kate McKinnon

Leslie Venturoso
MRAW Power Puff

11° Miyuki Delicas:

159
712 F
1054

Eileen Montgomery
Nine Wing Ring / MRAW Power Puff section

Eileen swatched a bit of a Power Puff using our MRAW Bellyband start. When we first made this open start to the Puff Rope, we thought of it as a Nine-Wing Ring...

Beads used:
11° Miyuki Delicas:

250	690
254	793
371	795
653	798

Mary Ruth Gray
Bow-Tie Necklace

Mary Ruth's necklet features two Power Puffs, a bit of Kumihimo rope, and a magnetic clasp.

Beads used:
11° Miyuki Delicas:

22 L
377

Maria Cristina Grifone

A beautiful Power Puff Bangle with no connecting tube. A bangle like this can be strung on sturdy beading wire or silk ribbon as easily as sewn together as a tube. *Photo by Francesca Pavoni.*

Beads used:
11° Miyuki Delicas:

10
166
281
923

Cate Jones
Pyramid Bangle

Cate used 11° Miyuki Delica for her Pyramids:

981

Pyramids & Tetrahedrons

Both Cate Jones and Christina Vandervlist brought 3-D triangle bracelets to the table for this book. Our instructions combine their techniques.

Cate's Pyramids have square bases, as Pyramids should, and Christina's Tetrahedrons have triangular bases. You already know how to get these started (see pg. 50 for the Flat Peyote Triangle pattern, and pg. 28 for a Simple Flat Square).

Experiment with different base shapes, decreases and stepped increases.

Christina's Tetrahedrons were made with 11° Miyuki Delicas:

144
459
507

and 11° Toho Aikos:
85
866

Dustin Wedekind's *Stepped Bowl* (below) employs the same peyote technique as Christina's Tetrahedrons (above and opposite, bottom) but the math is a bit different. The bowl features four rounds of increase for every pair of Point and Fill Rounds, while the Tetrahedrons alternate equal rounds of Point, Fill and Decrease (see pattern, pg. 86).

How could you resist combining these elements into fabulous neckpieces that cascade over your collarbones in explosions of Dodecahedromids, Pyragons, and Trianglospheres? The architects in us sing out at the possibilities.

Right: Dustin used 11° Miyuki Delicas for his triangular bowl:

02
03
371
390
760

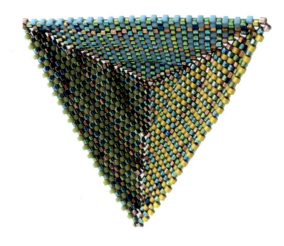

Pyramids

Left: begin with a Simple Flat Square (see pg. 28).

If you want flat shapes to stay flat, mind your tension: if it's too tight, the base may twist or cup. It may also help to work your Square flat on a tabletop and press the beadwork down as you pull the thread through.

Round 1   Fill Round: Peyote 1 bead in each space.

Round 2:   Decrease: Peyote 1 bead in each side space and pull together the "shoulder" beads in each corner.

Round 3:   Point Round: Peyote 1 bead in each side space and 1 bead in each corner.

Round 4:   Fill Round: Peyote 1 bead in each side space.

Round 5:   Decrease: Peyote 1 bead in each side space and pull together the "shoulder" beads in each corner.

Round 6:   Point Round: Peyote 1 bead in each side space and 1 bead in each corner.

Round 7:   Fill Round: Peyote 1 bead in each side space.

Round 8:   Decrease: Peyote 1 bead in each side space and pull together the "shoulder" beads in each corner.

Round 9:   Point Round: Peyote 1 bead in each side space and 1 bead in each corner.

Round 10:   Fill Round: Peyote 1 bead in each side space.

Round 11:   Decrease: Peyote 1 bead in each side space and pull together the "shoulder" beads in each corner.

Round 12:   Close the Pyramid: Peyote 1 bead in each corner.

Materials: medium weight beading thread (we used Nymo B)
2 g. 11° cylinder beads

Technique: circular peyote

Tension: moderate to snug

Difficulty: You can do it!

Diagrams read left to right, by line. The base is shown in grey for a few rounds to help you visualize the 3-D structure.

Rounds 1 - 3

4 - 6

7 - 9

10 - 12

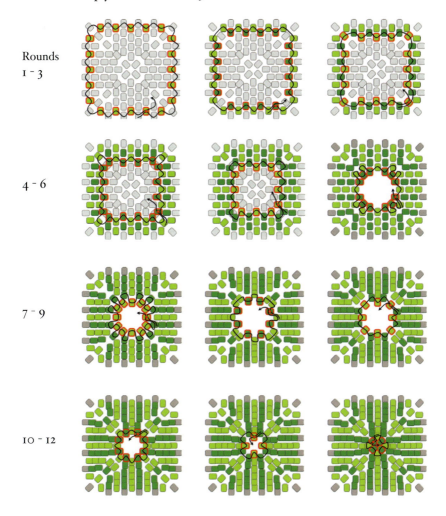

Contemporary Geometric Beadwork by Kate McKinnon

Tetrahedrons

Tetrahedron Base

Build a Flat Peyote Triangle until each side is 7 beads. Add a Point Round.

Tetrahedron Top

Round 1:   Fill Round: Peyote 1 bead in each space.

Round 2:   Decrease: Peyote 1 bead in each side space and pull together the "shoulder" beads in each corner.

Round 3:   Point Round: Peyote 1 bead in each side space and 1 bead in each corner.

Round 4:   Fill Round: Peyote 1 bead in each side space.

Round 5:   Decrease: Peyote 1 bead in each side space and pull together the "shoulder" beads in each corner.

Materials: same as Pyramids, previous page.

Tetrahedron Top, continued

Round 6 and Up:

Repeat Rounds 3 through 5 until you complete the Tetrahedron element. To make a Geometric Rope with them, stop before you close the form completely, and begin a bit of tube to the next element.

If you want a connected chain of Tetrahedrons, you have plenty of options; run beading wire through them, sew them together, or put them on wires or soldered mechanisms. There are quite a few channels and angles to choose from.

For a simple bracelet, it's easy to sew the elements to closed metal rings. Make the beaded loops big enough to move freely on the rings, and connect the clasp element with a sturdy jump ring.

Above: Tetrahedron Bracelet, Christina Vandervlist

Hidden Clasp

This clever little clasp is almost invisible when fully closed.

To make a hidden clasp for a Tetrahedron bracelet or necklace, create a little triangular snap-on base for one of them.

To do this, make a Flat Peyote Triangle four rounds larger than the base of your completed Tetrahedron. Bead a Point Round and a Fill Round, and follow with one Decrease Round.

Sew half of a dressmaker's snap into the inside of the top, and the other half onto the base of the Tetrahedron. To modify this clasp to work with the Pyramids, simply begin with a Simple Flat Square (pg. 28).

JoAnn Baumann

JoAnn made a Pyramid Bangle in a rainbow of related colours. (Those Delica numbers aren't randomly assigned, you know...) Her square clasp echoes the base of the pyramids, as Cate's triangular one (pg. 82) plays on the shape of the sides.

Beads used:
11° Miyuki Delicas:

10	722
651	723
658	724
661	730
721	733

"Colour is the place where our brain and the universe meet."

Paul Klee

Contemporary Geometric Beadwork by Kate McKinnon 89

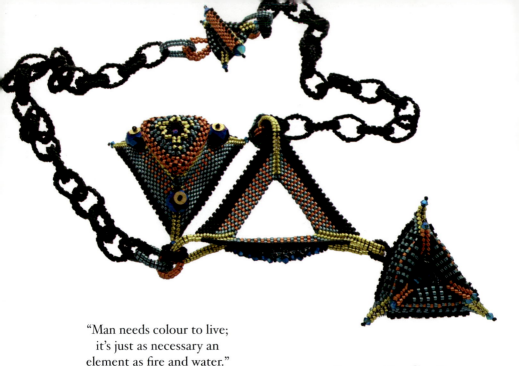

"Man needs colour to live; it's just as necessary an element as fire and water."

Fernand Léger

Jeannette Cook

It was wonderful to see these two pieces arrive in the mail, similar in concept but utterly different in execution.

Jeannette created a series of forms that unfold to reveal a glittering crystal. Her chain is beaded.

Barb's pendant is a lively interpretation of Christina Vandervlist's tidy *Triptych Pocket*, done in a hot mix of oranges, reds and turquoise, and finished with chains worked in both metal and beads.

See more views of this complex piece in our companion eBook.

"All men have stars, but they are not the same things for different people. For some, who are travelers, the stars are guides. For others they are no more than little lights in the sky. For others, who are scholars, they are problems..."

Antoine de Saint-Exupéry

Barb Linkert

"Space has always been the spiritual dimension of architecture.

It is not the physical statement of the structure so much as what it contains that moves us."

Arthur Erickson

Wings & Horns

When we found Wings we flew, and when we found Horns we built rocketships and space pods and freakishly beautiful flowers. What fun we had, discovering these forms. After a year of play, we've only just begun to think through (much less beadily explore) the possibilities. Our sketchbooks explode with delight, our beads quiver in their containers.

Above: A detail shot of Gabriella van Diepen's stunning cuff *The Devil's Eggs Are Hatching*, photo by Jeroen Medema.

Opposite, top: A view of a ManyHorn Bangle made by Cate Jones. See this piece also on pg. 135. Photo by Cate.

Opposite, bottom: the breakthrough *Eve's Thorns* cuff, also by Gabriella, photo by Jeroen. We'd been dancing around the idea of Horns for months, thinking about the relationship between Wings and Corners, but it was Gabri who raced it into town, like a vintage convertible coming down from a really good mountain road. (With champagne at breakfast.) See more of *Eve's Thorns* on pg. 118.

Rayo Boursier

Beads used:
11° Miyuki Delicas:

281
377
759
1152
1691

Our simple Tri-Wing soared into extravagant Winged and Horned forms. People sent beadwork from all over the world. The more we explored these forms, the further we wanted to take them.

Some pieces came out very stiff, some soft as water. It wasn't just about tension. Bead size, shape and finish were influencing form in unexpected ways. We tried a hundred things, but thousands called us.

"Perfection is achieved not when there
is nothing more to add, but when there
is nothing left to take away."

Antoine de Saint-Exupéry

Shelley Gross

Beads used:
11° Miyuki Delicas:

551
653
654
659

"Colour in certain places has the great value of making outlines and structural planes seem more energetic."

Antonio Gaudi

Cate Jones

Pink Pinstripe Rufflecuff

Beads used:
11° Miyuki Delicas:

4
1340

Kate McKinnon

Raven Cuff
Beads used:
8° gloss Toho rounds

Gabriella van Diepen

Lady Liberty Cuff, finished with leather

Beads used: 11° orange seed beads
and 11° Miyuki Delicas:

184
513
618
1012
1607 F

Dustin Wedekind
& Kate McKinnon

Wood Between The Worlds Bangle

Beads used:
11° Miyuki Delicas:

02
254 hex
371
753
879
1061

"...once you have tasted flight
you will walk the earth
with your eyes turned skywards,
for there you have been
and there you will long to return."

Leonardo da Vinci

Every choice we made in our Winged and Horned pieces gave different results. We tried round, triangle and drop beads in the Bellybands. We layered Wings and raised Horns in all of our forms, and each of them started with the ideas shown either in the Power Puff (pg. 56) or the Tri-Wing Ring (pg. 100).

See another view of the *Wood Between The Worlds* bangle on pg. 109.

Kate McKinnon

Above: *Sea Mistress Cuff*

Below: *Flying Three-Wing*
(see this piece also on pg. 108)

"Tension is the great integrity."

Buckminster Fuller

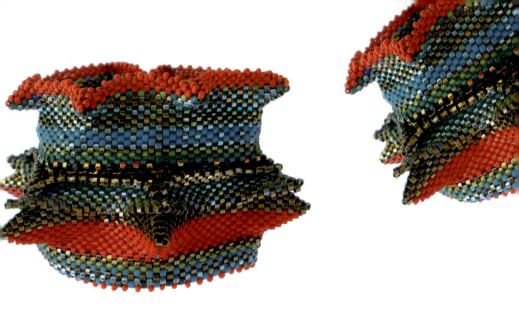

These pieces were Kate's first explorations of how Wings turn into Horns, or connect to form elements such as tube. Don't the 11° Toho triangles look lovely as the "verticals" in the MRAW Bellyband on the *Sea Mistress*? And can you see the dichroic Aiko 11° cylinders sparkling in the Band of the *Sea Monster*, above?

In the photograph of the starting curl of the Sea *Monster*, note the pagoda-like stacked square form that Winged pieces like these assume when they're built flat, instead of as bangles. The Sea Serpents (pgs. 128-132) do the same.

To make layered Horns, like you see on the *Monster*, begin a new increase before fully decreasing the first set of Horns. Once any Horn decrease is established, even just one row, the piece is willing to be round.

Black Elk says,

"Everything tries to be round."

Kate McKinnon
Sea Monster Cuff

Contemporary Geometric Beadwork by Kate McKinnon

Tri-Wing Ring

The Tri-Wing is built on our lovely MRAW Bellyband, and was the first piece we created with it. This adorable little element makes a ring, a chain link, and a perfect little maquette with which to swatch colours or patterns for larger pieces. Sized up and zipped together, it's a bangle.

The ideas behind the Tri-Wing don't stop at three sides. This versatile band can begin any shape or form, and offers both a quick start and an outrageously useful architecture for both structure and embellishment.

Both pages: Tri-Wing Rings by Dustin Wedekind and Kate McKinnon.

"It is not the beauty of a building you should look at first; it is the construction of the foundation that will stand the test of time."

David Allan Coe

The Tri-Wing is great practice for learning to make a snug Bellyband. It's best to get comfortable with the ideas presented here, in a small piece, before moving on to Horns, a Fortuneteller Bangle, or more dimensional Winged pieces. Once you can whip out a Tri-Wing with a nice snug Band and a bit of attitude on the corners, frankly, you're ready for anything.

Increases can be placed at any point in the peyote stitch, so stagger the points if you like, or add more or fewer corners. Place three increases for a triangular opening on one side of the Band, and four or five for a square or pentagonal opening on the other. Simply decide how many corners you want, and place that many increases.

You can scallop the edges (just skip the beads you don't want to add by passing through), zip them together, or add more sets of Wings coming straight off of the Bellyband. You can place Helix Points (see pg. 196), or decrease a set of Wings into Horns. (And if you do *that*, and increase again, you will find that, ta-da, you are making Geometric Rope, or a Power Puff Bangle.)

Below right, Eileen Montgomery's *Nine-Wing Ring* shows that the Winged Rings are clearly cross-sections of Power Puff Rope, but they are started from a Bellyband, not a Flat Peyote Triangle. Below left is a pretty scalloped Tri-Wing by Dustin Wedekind.

Choose your start based on the look you want, and your feelings regarding unbeading to open a tube in your Rope (see Finishing Geometric Rope Bangles, pg. 79, for more on this).

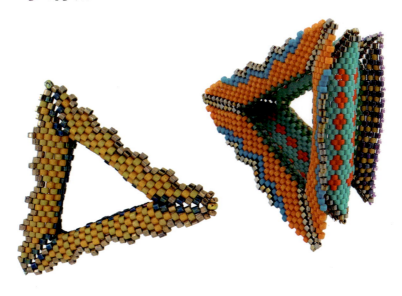

Contemporary Geometric Beadwork by Kate McKinnon

Tri-Wing Ring

All you need to know about making Wings from an MRAW Bellyband is here, in this simple element. Make a couple to the pattern and then... fly.

"Beauty is the first test: there is no permanent place in the world for ugly mathematics."

Godfrey Hardy

Our perky sample uses 11° Miyuki Delicas:

(A) 753 Matte Brick Red (bellyband)
(B) 798 Royal Blue (bellyband and peyote)
(C) 254 Bronze Hex (bellyband and ribs)
(D) 653 Pumpkin (peyote)
(E) 654 Brick Red (peyote, second side)

1. Planning Your Start: Sizing

Sizing beady rings is an imprecise science, because so much depends on the beads chosen and the tension you use, but we can offer some general guidelines.

Our sample is a size 6, and our Bellyband has 27 units. It's easiest to count spacer beads, which also handily number 27 (6 gold hex and 21 blue).

If you want the triangle to have even sides (not a requirement) keep the total number of Band units divisible by 3. So for each size up you go, add three units (which will add three blue spacer beads per side).

If you don't mind the triangle being eccentric, feel free to add units in any number to size the Tri-Wing up.

Materials:	medium weight beading thread (we used Nymo B) 5 g. of 11° cylinder beads 1 g. of 11° or 15° seed beads for edging (optional)
Techniques:	MRAW Bellyband, circular peyote, herringbone
Tension:	snug
Difficulty:	You can do it! Start with the Flat Peyote Triangle.

2. Make A Bellyband

If this is your first time making our MRAW Bellyband, you might enjoy our full RAW and MRAW Band tutorials in the Basics section, pages 38-39. Our MRAW Band is done with an elegant thread path that combines a full spacer round with a RAW band. This gives you both a lovely lot of structure for only one round of beading *and* a wonderful architectural support.

We used (A), (B) and (C) beads for our 27-unit band.

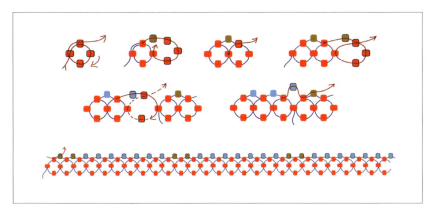

Remember, thread path is important for tailoring. Pass through the spacer beads only once, when you add them, and be certain to bypass them in the same way each time. Control the thread at all times to ensure a tight weave (we simply hold it down with our fingers until it's time to pull a stitch snug, then we trap it again).

Check the band for fit before joining; it should be a little loose on your finger, as it will tighten up a bit as you add increases. Your tension and thread control affect the fit, but remember bead style and size factor in too. Happily, most of us have ten fingers. (And friends with fingers.)

Tri-Wing Ring

3. Build Your Ring

Using circular peyote stitch, add 1(D) bead in each space, except for where you decide to place increases. In each of those spaces, place 2(C) beads. They will be the base of each herringbone rib.

For our size 6 sample, we placed 3 increases of 2(C) beads each, separated by 8 single (D) bead adds, and our round band of beads became a triangle.

Here are two views of the first round added to the joined Bellyband.

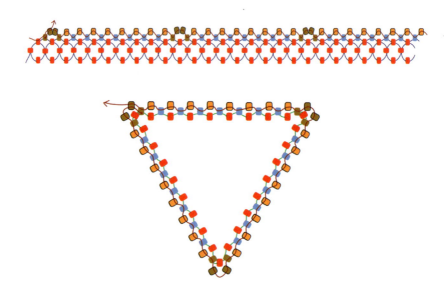

When you finish the round, remember to "step up" by passing through the first bead or beads added in the round, placing your needle in position to begin a new round.

As you can see in the illustrations above, we began our round with our first two-bead increase, and now that the triangular form has snapped into being, our step-up is the first of two corner beads, with the thread exiting between the pair.

If you would prefer your step-up to be in the middle of a side (so it's easier to see) instead of in a corner, simply needle through the work until you are at the point at which you'd like to place your step-up.

The process of adding two beads in each corner space is the same as in the Flat Peyote Triangle, which is why we recommend beginning with it (see pg. 50). Instead of working flat, however, or making a closed form like a Puff, you are now creating dimensional space, building out into the air (or beginning a "Z" axis, if you enjoy thinking that way).

In the illustration below, our thread is exiting between two corner beads. To continue the herringbone increase, we will pick up 2(C) beads, pass back down through the second corner bead, and then add 1(D) bead in each space until we reach the next corner.

Continue adding rounds, stacking your two-bead increases at the corners, until the first set of Wings are the desired length.

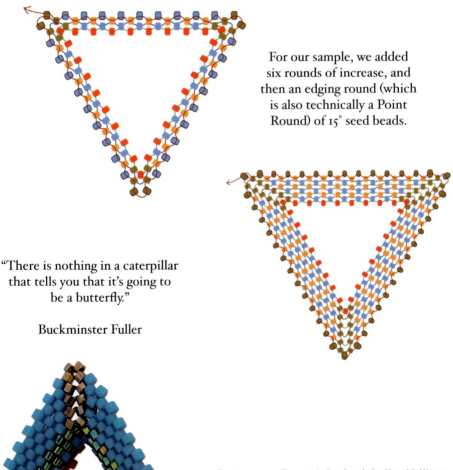

For our sample, we added six rounds of increase, and then an edging round (which is also technically a Point Round) of 15° seed beads.

"There is nothing in a caterpillar that tells you that it's going to be a butterfly."

Buckminster Fuller

Contemporary Geometric Beadwork by Kate McKinnon   105

Tri-Wing Ring

Add A Second Side

When the first side is completed and edged, needle back to the other side of the Bellyband, and add a second side of Wings by repeating the steps used to make the first. As this side of the Band has no spacers, you will need to put in an extra round if you want the height of the Wings on each side of the Band to match.

To make our sample, we added three rounds of (E) beads on our second side, and an edging round of Toho 15° seed beads.

You may wish to pass back through some or all of your beadwork to reinforce the rounds or increase the tension. We generally take a reinforcing pass through our edge rounds, but focus on building the work itself sturdily enough to stand with one pass.

The thread used will have much to do with whether or not you need to reinforce your stitches. We use Nymo, which allows us (if it suits us) to deliberately pass through previous threads to join and weave together the thread inside our beads. This does wonders for both longevity and tailoring, and helps somewhat to mitigate the "single running thread" weakness of peyote stitch.

Pearl Of Wisdom

As noted in the Flat Peyote Triangle pattern, a common error when learning geometric circular peyote is missing the first or last bead adds of each side of a round, just under the rib increases. This potential for error becomes much stronger when you move from flat to dimensional pieces.

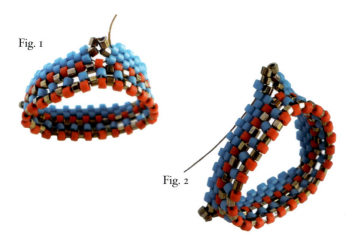

Fig. 1

Fig. 2

In Fig 1, above, another blue bead needs to be added before the side is completed and the needle enters the bronze rib bead. The peyote stitch climbs the herringbone, providing little slots on each side of each new two-bead add for new beads, but the end spaces can be tricky to spot.

As when learning the Triangle or the Power Puff, it can be very helpful to set out the beads needed for each side or round before you begin it, so that if you do have an error, you will only have one round to unbead. Once comfortable with the technique, you will be able to see right away when a bead is needed, or when it's time to step up.

In Fig. 2, you can see the same corner, one round later, with the adds next to the rib beads completed.

Three-Wing

Experimenting with Numbers of Wings

Above: A triple-layer Flying Three-Wing with two of the three layers zipped together in three runs to make a few sections of tube for the forged bronze frame. See another view of this piece on page 98.

Below: Four-Wings are never still. They flex and dance and must be persuaded to remain flat. Adding a round of Horns (by decreasing one set of Wings) works well for squaring them up, but allowing them to move makes them more fun to wear. Both pieces on this page by Kate.

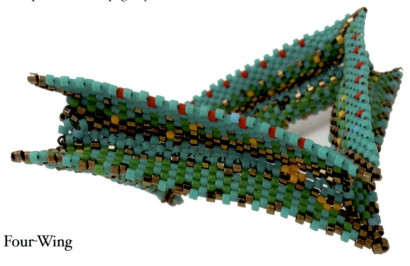

Four-Wing

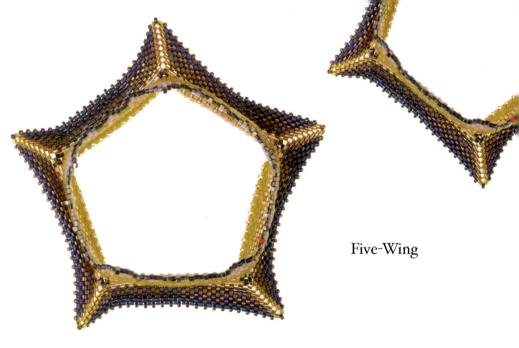

Five-Wing

Above: Five-Wings are very stable, and accept their shape from their first round of increase. Starfishy beadwork by Gabriella van Diepen.

Below: The Wood Between the Worlds Six-Wing, beaded by Dustin and Kate, was one of our real "Aha!" moments making the book. Dustin had set it aside, as the eccentric shape seemed unmanageable, twisting and turning, not wanting to round out. Kate picked it up to play with the idea of Horns, and after the first round of decrease it settled willingly into a flat shape and was stable. It's now one of the most enjoyable pieces to wear. See another view of this piece on pg. 97.

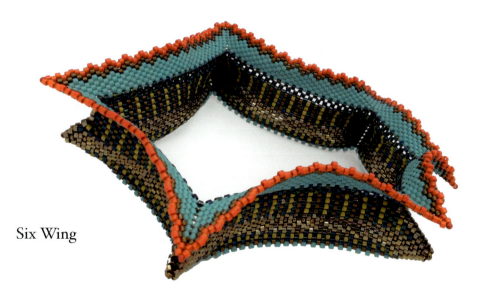

Six Wing

Decreasing or Tailoring Wings

Straps and Bands

One of the simplest ways to have Wings mimic Horns is to sew a strip or a band across them, or a little wave of beads. You can tailor pieces quite nicely by doing this. It's also a great tactic to size a piece radically down; just build a bangle of the right size on top of the one that isn't, or on either side of one that isn't. The top round of peyote stitch is a Toothrow, and it's always ready for more peyote or a RAW or an MRAW band.

Above: Kate McKinnon built this cuff an inch too big and then sized it down with little straps on one side and a flowy blue river on the other.

Right: Some very neatly done tailoring by Kim Boeckman. The flat, round band is a perfect accompaniment to the spiky Horns and Wings.

But if you prefer Horns...real Horns...

turn the page.

Turning Wings Into Horns

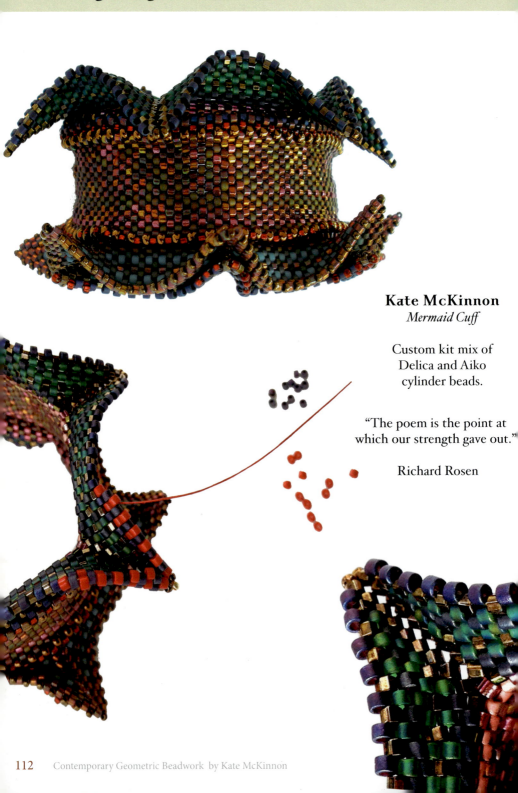

Kate McKinnon
Mermaid Cuff

Custom kit mix of Delica and Aiko cylinder beads.

"The poem is the point at which our strength gave out."

Richard Rosen

Peyote Decrease

A regular peyote corner decrease on the wingtips will give you a delightful puffy pointy tip, just as when making a Power Puff (see Decreasing a Triangle Into a Puff, pg. 58).

The Wing-to-Horn decrease is *exactly like* the corner decrease you already know how to do. Simply place a Point Round at the final height of your Wings (Kate got fancy and did a little 3-bead picot for the tips of her Mer-wings) and then add a Fill Round.

At that point, just like in the triangular Puff, you are set to begin to decrease. Practice your moves on the Power Puff Ring (pg. 62) or the Caldera Bangle (pg. 72).

In the photo below, you can see that we are giving the single set of Wings on the Mermaid Cuff some spanky red Underhorns. We're going back into the finished piece to do it, but Horns can happen quite naturally at any time you wish to begin a decrease in a piece. You'll see them popping out simply everywhere in the pieces in the following pages.

Tinyhorn Bangle (with removable bellyband)

Making a Tinyhorn is the simplest way to learn about Horn structure and placement. It starts out just like a Tri-Wing Ring, with an MRAW Bellyband. A nice twist to this piece is that the Bellyband is removable and re-usable. Having a starter Band in your beadbox is an easy way to save the time spent starting and get straight to beading.

Build a Band that will be able to go over your hand after the Wings and Horns tighten it up. Use a bangle sizer to figure it out. Adding Horns really tailors the piece inward (for a smaller bangle) so the starting Band should be about an inch bigger than the desired finished size, depending on your tension and how you like bangles to fit.

The mighty Bangle Sizer should be in your beadbox.

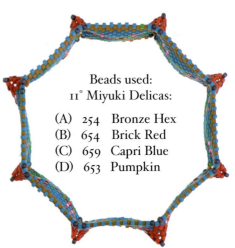

Beads used:
11° Miyuki Delicas:

(A) 254 Bronze Hex
(B) 654 Brick Red
(C) 659 Capri Blue
(D) 653 Pumpkin

114   Contemporary Geometric Beadwork by Kate McKinnon

Materials: medium beading thread (we used Nymo B)
approx. 30 g. of 11° cylinder beads

Technique: removable MRAW Bellyband, Wings, Horns, circular peyote

Tension: snug

Difficulty: You can do it! Start with a Tri-Wing Ring.

Removable Bellyband

Step 1: Make and join a MRAW Bellyband to your size. Our sample is very small, and began with 88 units. This start, divided by 8, gives our Tinyhorn eight 11-bead sides. After your Band is joined, add a peyote round on the side with no spacers.

Step 2: Needle back to the first side, and take a reinforcing pass through the first round of spacers. Weave in your starting and ending threads, but leave the tails sticking out a little bit, so you can see them.

Begin the Tinyhorn on Top of the Band

Step 3: Cut three new threads (we like to use a bright colour for these, like red Nymo) about 6" long each. Use all three of them (each one for a third of the Band circumference) to place a new round of peyote on one side of the Band.

Use these three threads loosely, and leave the tails long. You'll pull all three of them out once the Tinyhorn is built, or once you have at least five rounds on, and the re-usable Band will be separated from the bangle. (Or, of course, you can keep the Band... read on.)

Contemporary Geometric Beadwork by Kate McKinnon   115

Tinyhorn Bangle (with removable bellyband)

Step 3: Add another 4 rounds of plain circular peyote. (Note that the thread overlaps are drawn closer together than they will be in your bangle.)

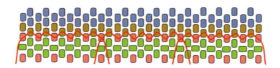

Step 4: Place your increases in the 6th round. Our sample used an 88-unit Band, and we chose an octagonal shape. This meant we placed our eight two-bead increases in every eleventh space. The round in which you place your increases is the point at which the piece becomes dimensional. Within one round's worth of adds, your piece moves from this:

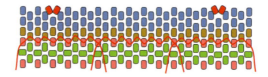

To this (spaces exaggerated to show their eventual position):

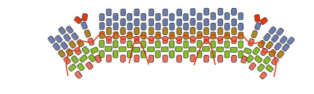

Like mapmakers, we gave a lot of thought to how to diagram Horns, and we decided to show all of them in mirror-image exploded drawings. If you zipped them together in 3-D space, the Wings would form Horns. In fact, that is another way to make them, simply zip two Winged forms together. (Just like closing a Power Puff or Caldera Bangle...)

Step 5: Increase for a total of four rounds to form Wings, place a Point Round, a Fill Round, and decrease for three rounds to form Horns. Work five more rounds of plain peyote to match the start.

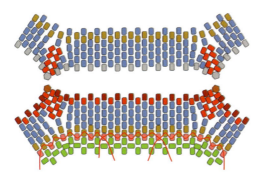

Step 6: When you pull the three threads, the two sections will separate and the re-usable Bellyband and Tinyhorn will be separate pieces. Needle down to your beginning round, and take a reinforcing pass. Weave in your tails, or add an edging.

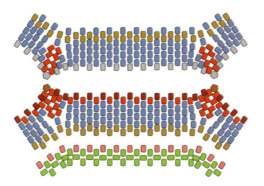

The Bellyband can also remain in the piece and you can build more Horns on the other side of it, as we do in our Horned Melon Bangles (pg. 120).

Gabriella van Diepen

Eve's Thorns

Below left and above: details of Gabriella's extraordinary Horned Bangle *Eve's Thorns* (also on pg. 92). The turquoise tips on each Horn slay us with their beady perfection.

One of the things we love to do is to stare at our beadwork, absorbing the patterns and the structure, and then try to visualize alternate paths, ask questions. What if key elements were worked in different colours or counts?

Imagine, if you dare, Gabriella's repeating RAW bands in bright green, or an inner layer rising up inside one of these hot red pieces in stripes of turquoise and orange, or a sweep of shimmering silver.

Photos of Gabriella's bangles by Jeroen Medema.

More Horned Delights

Horned Bangles were thrilling forms that happened in a great wave when we all caught Horn Fever. (There is no cure. Read this section advisedly.)

The Horn excitement began when Gabriella examined an early piece of Kate's called the *Digital Cuff* (detail in the circle below) which sported tiny proto-UnderHorns, and then she made the beautiful *Devil Never Walks Alone* cuff (below). Suddenly Horns were exploding onto every surface of our work, even our Rick-Rack Bangles.

Gabriella van Diepen

The Devil Never Walks Alone

Left, a detail of the first little Underhorns we discovered on the Digital Cuff.

Gabri just suddenly *realized* that the Wings could be decreased just like corners; that in fact all of our Wingtips were, by definition, potential corners. We had to sit down.

Horned Melon Bangle

Kim Boeckman

11° Miyuki Delicas:
131
371
505
771
794

11° Toho round
seed beads:
PF-564F

and 15° Miyuki
round seed beads:
291J
318Q

This beautiful Horned Melon version by Kim Boeckman is a study in subtle plays of colour, bead shape and size. We love the 11° pink Japanese rounds she used in her Bellyband (so delightfully regular) and the little fizz of hot pink 15° rounds on top of her upper layer of Horns. Kim says,

> "The colors in this bracelet were inspired by the view outside of my studio during the drought of summer. Every growing thing was dry and seemingly lifeless, except one little bunch of flowers near the water spigot…those flowers were pink."

This Horned Melon began with a Bellyband of 90 units.

After several rounds of plain peyote on each side of the Band, two-bead increases were placed in every 10th space, leaving 9 beads in between them, and the twenty resulting Horns grew in the top and bottom rounds. Staggering them like a turned dial was a nice touch visually.

Kim increased for five rounds for the bottom Horns and three rounds for those on top, and finished her edges with 15° rounds.

Vary this piece by randomizing the Horns, playing with the colours, Horn placement, and bead counts.

It's easy to see what a profound Shrinking effect the Horns have on general tailoring when you compare the 90 unit starting band (which is large for a plain bangle) to the eventual bangle, which is for a medium hand (about 8").

Remember this sizing tip if you ever have a bangle that is growing too big. Horns work like darts in fabric to take things in, inside out 3-D glass darts. How fabulous is that?

Increase Kim's pattern in increments of 9 Bellyband units to size up, but remember, different beads will make different sizes, as will different numbers of Horns. Experiment with your bead selection by making a Winged Ring that has the same spacing between increases that you plan to use in your bangle.

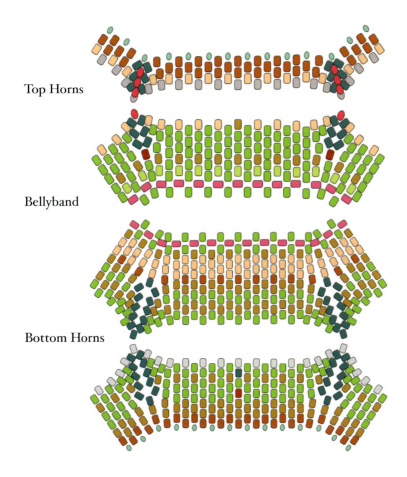

Top Horns

Bellyband

Bottom Horns

Contemporary Geometric Beadwork by Kate McKinnon

Kim Boeckman
Horned Melon

Beads used:
11° Miyuki Delicas:
131
371
505
771
794

11° Toho rounds:
PF-564F

15° Miyuki rounds:
299J
318Q

"By the work one knows the workman."

Jean de La Fontaine

Jenni Gerstle
Horned Melon

Beads used:
11° Miyuki Delicas:

12	1064
377	1135
391	1491
876	1838
1052	

15° Toho rounds
A503

"Above all, the color is the liberation, perhaps even more so than the drawing."

Henri Matisse

Kate McKinnon
First Horned Melon

Beads used:
11° Miyuki Delicas:

custom blue and grey mix
254 hex
791

11° Toho rounds:
457

Maria Cristina Grifone

Pagoda Bangle
photo by Francesca Pavoni

Beads used:
11° Miyuki Delicas:
157
168
310

"The architecture of a story can be a little bit different if it's a true story."

Joel Coen

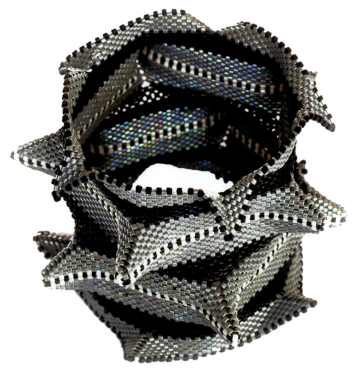

Contemporary Geometric Beadwork by Kate McKinnon

Advanced variations and Gallery pieces are not stepped out line by line, but are presented simply as colour listings and, in some cases, as diagrams that show the pattern counts. Study how the pieces go together, maybe change the math, the colourways, or the size a little bit. We are simply agog to see what you whip up. We hope that you double down on everything; make fantastical shapes.

The eBook version of this book is alive, and has room for limitless galleries of work and links to your own sites, books, and patterns. We're interested in your counts, colourways, your Wing and Horn placements, all of your crazed creations. After all, for so many reasons, we don't want to end up to be Georg Baselitz...

"I paint German artists whom I admire. I paint their pictures, their work as painters, and their portraits too. But oddly enough, each of these portraits ends up as a picture of a woman with blonde hair. I myself have never been able to work out why this happens."

Georg Baselitz

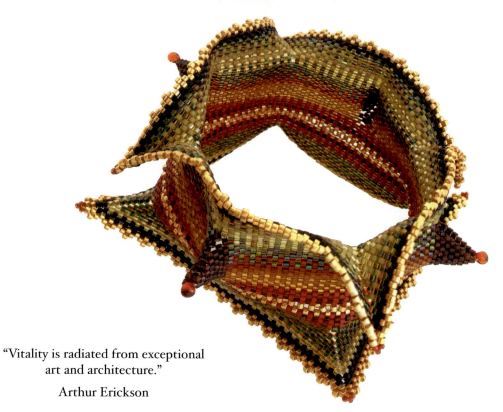

"Vitality is radiated from exceptional art and architecture."

Arthur Erickson

Kelly Angeley

Hornwing

Beads used:
11° Miyuki Delicas:

310
378
390
909
1391
1392
1681
1684
1741
1833

Pomegranate drops
397I

Turquoise Hornwing

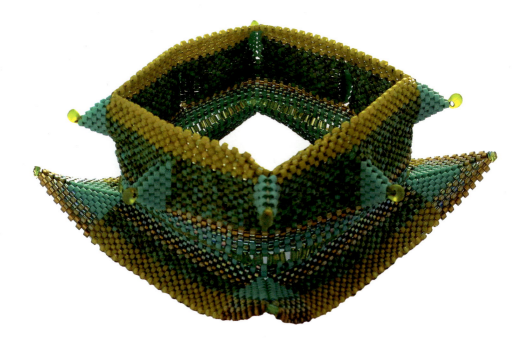

To make this beautiful piece, Kelly began with an MRAW Bellyband of 88 units. For the Band, she used 11° Toho Triangles and 11° Toho Aiko cylinders in turquoise. For the MRAW spacers, she chose gold-lined aqua. In these beads, her 88-unit starting band worked up to be a 9" bangle.

She wanted an even square, so she planned for four rounds of increase by choosing a number of Band units that was divisible by four. She placed her four two-bead increases at every 22nd space in the first round of peyote.

Wings and Horns can grow to whatever height you wish. In this piece, Kelly's Wings soar to 24 rounds, with an underrow of neat little Horns that are each five rounds long. She tipped each Wing and Horn with hand-etched Magatama drops.

Be sure to calculate your bracelet size based on actual beads used. For example, using all matte Delicas might have resulted in the piece being as much as a half-inch smaller overall.

Kelly Angeley

Beads used:
11° Toho Aikos:
246
369
413
995
999
2051

11° Toho Treasures
307

11° Toho Triangles
(Bellyband verticals)
393

12 Magatama or other drops for tips

Golden-Horned Sea Serpent

Gabriella van Diepen

Photos by Jeroen Medema
Beads used:
24k gold and silver Delica
and Aiko mix

"A mind that is stretched by a new experience can never go back to its old dimensions."

Oliver Wendell Holmes, Jr.

> "The purpose of art is washing the dust of daily life off our souls."
>
> Pablo Picasso

The Golden-Horned Sea Serpent is a long wrap bracelet. It curls naturally, but we enhanced the grab with an addition of memory wire. We chose a medium-weight wire, which is strong enough to keep the piece on your arm, but soft enough to let you wear it around your neck as well.

Golden-Horned Sea Serpent

1. Make an MRAW Bellyband long enough to wrap 3 or 4 times around your arm.

2. Bead 7 rounds of plain peyote and an edge finish on one side of the band. Gabriella used a silvery mix of Delica and Aiko cylinder beads, and 15° rounds for the edge.

3. Add three rounds of plain peyote on the other side of the band. Gabriella used a mix of golden Delica and Aiko cylinder beads.

4. Pop in a Guide Round (Fig. 1) for the memory wire to run through while it's easy to access. Choose sturdy beads with holes big enough for the wire. 10° cylinder beads or Japanese rounds work well. Thread the memory wire.

5. Return to the second side of the band, and add a round with increases where you want the Horns to grow. Gabri placed hers every 14-24 beads apart, and built her Wings to 7 rounds in height. Fig. 2 shows the entire pattern, exploded.

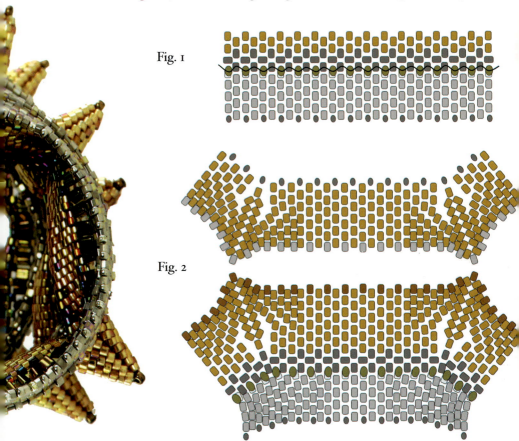

Fig. 1

Fig. 2

130   Contemporary Geometric Beadwork by Kate McKinnon

Gabriella van Diepen modelling her Golden-Horned Sea Serpent.
Photo by Jeroen Medema.

Sculptural work is fun to wear, and even the largest beadworked bangles are lightweight if they are built only with the beads themselves. Work gets heavy when it's backed with fabric, or holding solid glass or gems, but the little beads themselves are light as feathers.

The Sea Serpent may not be ideal for personal ornament while swabbing decks or knitting, but we suspect that you will find that wearing art jewelry out into the world excites other humans so much that it's well worth the minor inconvenience of remembering that you have it on.

Life is short; the more beauty we can spread, the better. And you may enjoy having strangers stop you on the streets and chat you up on trains. Who knows what adventures you will have when you take a creation like this out to the opera, or the grocery store?

Julie Glasser

Rainbow Sea Serpent

Beads used:
11° Miyuki Delicas:

10	658
160	659
164	1133
167	1371
169	1379
214	1573
253	1577

"Not everything that counts can be counted. Not everything that can be counted counts."

Albert Einstein

Christina Vandervlist

Right: A Fortuneteller Bangle (pattern on pg. 164) may be the ultimate expression of Horns and Wings, with the added excitement of having been built on a Zigged Band.

132   Contemporary Geometric Beadwork by Kate McKinnon

Helen Fountain

A Horned Melon bangle, accented with drop beads at edges and Horntips.

Beads used:
11° Miyuki Delicas:

04
614
615

11° Toho rounds:
375

Miyuki Drops:
DP 9003

"When I am working on a problem, I never think about beauty, but when I have finished, if the solution is not beautiful, I know it is wrong."

Buckminster Fuller

"Art is beauty, the perpetual invention of detail, the choice of words, the exquisite care of execution."

Théophile Gautier

Teresa Sullivan

Flaming Hornwing
photos by Kyle Cassidy

Beads used:
11° Miyuki Delicas:
 723
 727
 791

11° Czech red rounds
gold-filled wire

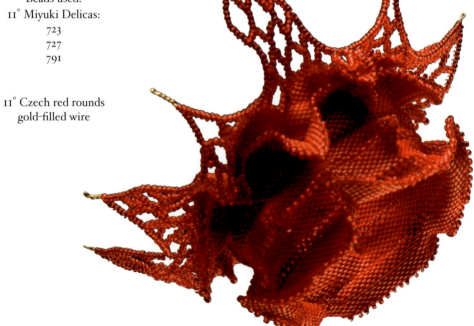

134   Contemporary Geometric Beadwork by Kate McKinnon

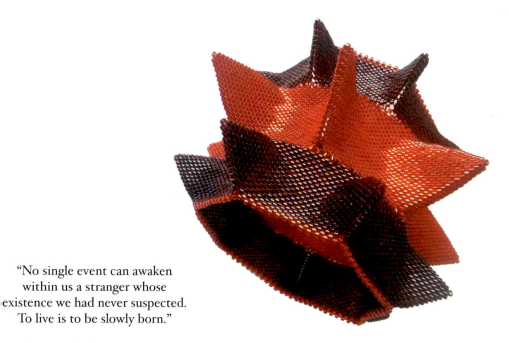

"No single event can awaken
within us a stranger whose
existence we had never suspected.
To live is to be slowly born."

Antoine de Saint-Exupéry

Cate Jones

Manyhorn
photos by Cate Jones

Beads used:
11° Miyuki Delicas:
297
602

Contemporary Geometric Beadwork by Kate McKinnon   135

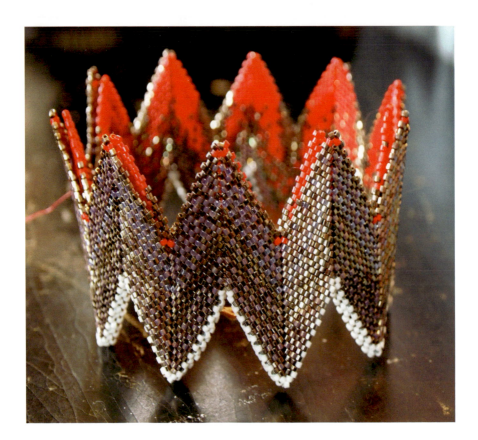

Rick ✦ Rack

The peyote Rick-Rack (or Zig-Zag) pattern can be made in a variety of ways. Traditionally, it's been worked from a long peyote start in which two rows are strung at once. In that start, increases and decreases can flip and mimic each other, and it can be easy to get confused about which side you are working on. People such as Gerlinde Lenz and Jean Power have devised elegant strategies to keep Zigs straight from Zags, and have made beautiful work.

We're excited to present an alternative beginning, one that offers a quick start with no confusion about which side you are beading, and gives you the option of easy layers: our exciting, architectural Zigged Bellyband. It can hold one or many rounds of beadwork, each of which can assume a variety of forms.

If you prefer the finished piece to be only plain peyote, but you love our start, you can bead a Removable Bellyband (see the Tinyhorn Bangle, pg. 114). If we kept only one starter Band in our beadboxes, it would be a Zigged one.

We hope you enjoy the simplicity of the Zigged start, as it's engaged us with great delight since the day we discovered it. We are excited to see what you create; we will thrill to your shapes and forms and Zigs and Zags.

If we had tried to make even a thousandth of the Rick-Racks, layered cuffs, Zigged Hornwings and Fortuneteller Bangles we've visualized, this book would never have been started, much less finished. We'd still be sitting in the garden, with roses growing round our heads, beading away. It's where we probably are, right now, working on the next volume or pattern.

Opposite: the *Red Queen Crown* (in progress) by Kate McKinnon. The Band for this crown was made in white, so you could see the structure.

Below: Rick-Rack is also the basis of the Winged and Horned Fortuneteller Bangle, in the magical hands of Larry Gatti, below and in that very garden.

Contemporary Geometric Beadwork by Kate McKinnon

Rick-Rack Bangle

"We shape our buildings; thereafter they shape us."

Winston Churchill

MRAW Zigged Bellyband

Our version of Rick-Rack begins with our magnificent MRAW Zigged Band (illustrated above joined into a bangle) after one round of beadwork (above left) and only two rounds (above right). That's a lot of structure for one and two rounds of beading. If you work snugly, and control the Band, it will zig and zag immediately.

The joined MRAW Zigged Band forms the base of the double-layered Rick-Rack Bangles on the opposite page. See it sitting there, at the bottom, orange and strong? (Beadwork by Ann Rishell.)

Grow each layer as tall as you like, even start new layers growing out of the other side of the Band. You are limited only by your imagination and, of course, your access to beads. (And you are going to need a LOT of beads.)

The photo below shows a strip of band worked flat (perfect for strap bracelets or hatbands). The Bellyband is on the bottom of the piece, with one side still soft and open, waiting for a finish or for another layer or layers. (Beadwork by Kate McKinnon.)

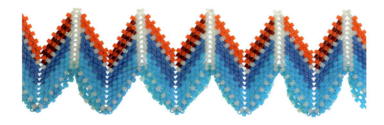

Rick-Rack Bangle

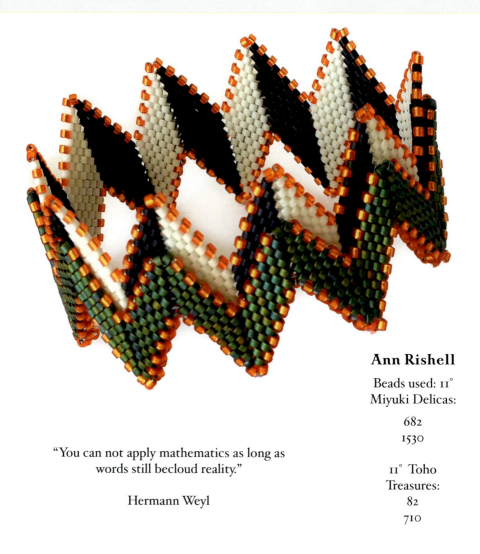

Ann Rishell

Beads used: 11° Miyuki Delicas:

682
1530

11° Toho Treasures:

82
710

"You can not apply mathematics as long as words still becloud reality."

Hermann Weyl

After two rounds of MRAW Zigging, you have architecture and structure, which we find thrilling.

Keep your thread snug in this start; you are building a foundation. It should be tight and tidy, with no gaps or extra space. Remember to pay attention to the direction in which you bypass the spacer beads; be consistent, as it will show in your tailoring. If this is your first Rick-Rack Bangle, you might consider making it flat at least until you are sure of the size you need. You can always join it after the shape firms up.

Materials:	medium weight beading thread (we used Nymo B) 20-50 g. of 11° cylinder beads
Techniques:	MRAW Zigged Bellyband, circular peyote, herringbone
Tension:	snug
Difficulty:	You can do it! Start with the Tri-Wing Ring.

Step 1: MRAW Zigged Band

Create a Zigged Band (see pgs. 42-43) placing your increases and decreases evenly in the spacer round. In our example, the increases and decreases are placed in every seventh space.

With the 11° cylinder beads we used, each Peak spans about 3/4", and the finished bangle fits the outside of the Bangle Sizer at the 6 3/4 mark; this is small for a slip-on bangle.

Divide your size by about 3/4" to determine how many Peaks you will need for fit, remembering that both tension and beads chosen will play into your final sizing.

Step 2: Peyote Zig-Zag

Build the inner layer of peyote zig-zag to the desired height, with two-bead increases on each Peak top and pass-through decreases at the bottoms. The number of beads per side, Peak, and round will remain the same as your Rick-Rack grows taller.

Repeat the peyote build on the unused side of the Zigged Band to bead the outer layer to the desired height. Finish the edges of your beadwork with drops, rounds, or leave them open to build more on later.

Contemporary Geometric Beadwork by Kate McKinnon

Rick-Rack Bangle

Left: holding a decrease together while the thread is pulled snug.

Above: holding an increase.

How you hold the growing beadwork has a great deal to do with how it behaves, and how much tension you can apply to the working thread.

By holding decreases together and keeping Zigs Zigged when you draw your thread snug, you encourage the structure to develop correctly and immediately.

We love Nymo B and D from the large cones for this work. If you use a slick thread, you might want to take a few circle-rounds around a bead or two every now and then to keep your tension metered. (Or try some lovely red Nymo from a cone.)

The Rick-Rack carries pattern beautifully. The band below was crafted by Danielle McElroy Brown.

The Zigged Band after one and two rounds.

"...a noble, logical diagram once recorded will not die."

Daniel Burnham

Contemporary Geometric Beadwork by Kate McKinnon

144 Contemporary Geometric Beadwork by Kate McKinnon

Above and below: double-layer swatches by Kate McKinnon.

Opposite top: a zipped reversible bangle, by Dustin Wedekind.

Opposite bottom: double-layered swatches by Kate McKinnon.

Christina Vasil

Beads used:
11° Miyuki Delicas:

29
201
362
768

11° Miyuki drops:
462D

Gabriella van Diepen

Night Circus

Beads used:
11° Miyuki Delicas:

310
410
635
795

"I try to apply colors like words that shape poems, like notes that shape music."

Joan Miro

146 Contemporary Geometric Beadwork by Kate McKinnon

Leslie Venturoso

Beads used:
11° Miyuki Delicas:

custom blue mix
331
377
504
1691

15° Toho rounds
457

Leslie Venturoso

Beads used:
11° Miyuki Delicas:

224
682
1832

"Why do two colors, put one next to the other, sing? Can one really explain this?"

Pablo Picasso

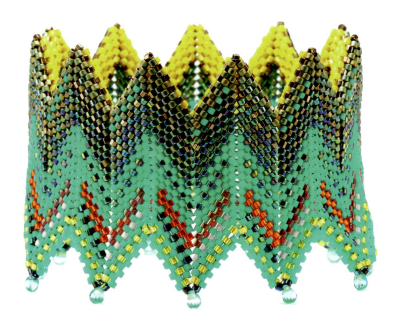

Above: An exciting piece by Gabriella van Diepen, with a hot yellow stabilizing strip as an inner layer. *Photo by Jeroen Medema.*

Below: Interesting double Rick-Rack by Kirsty Little.

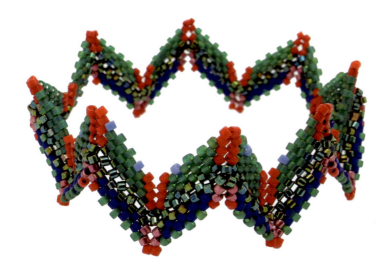

Above: The Bellyband can be a central element, but you have to decide about that when you begin adding the second layer. Either fold it under, for a double layer, or build it as an opposite of the first layer.

Below: A double-swatch by Kate McKinnon.

Bottom: Alma Legacy's lovely piece, using a clever start by Gerlinde Lenz.

Horned Rick-Rack

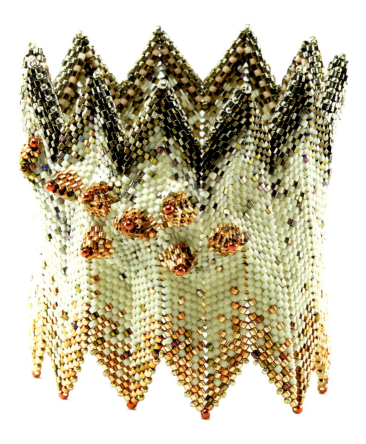

A close study of this beautiful Horned Rick-Rack cuff by Gabriella van Diepen will show that she took advantage of the MRAW Bellyband to add a small, stable reinforcing layer to one end of this piece. See it there, tucked up on the inside of the cuff at the top of the photo? This second layer is easiest to add when the piece is small, as shown on pg. 138.

With just those few double rows, the cuff remains elliptical and stiff enough to wear. Imagine the design possibilities of a second layer, though...think of an inside sleeve on this piece in a hot red. Or ocean blue.

This is an advanced piece, because it's a bit much to hold in your hands (and your mind) while the Horns are going together. Try one of these after making a Horned Melon or other Horned Bangle, and when you feel relaxed and comfortable with the Rick-Rack stitch.

Gabriella's little golden Horns explode like mountain ranges in the snowy, starry, fabric of her tall cuff, and they grow against the grain of the Rick-Rack weave. This is what makes their expansion hard to control with your hands. Making each Horn in gold beads helped her keep track of them, but it's still a bit chaotic as the bangle sprawls open with all of the Horn adds.

What Gabriella did with this first piece was as much like striking out across a mountain range as creating one; it was a pioneering moment in our design progression, and almost immediately inspired Christina to create the splendid Fortuneteller Bangle.

Photographs by Jeroen Medema.

Gabriella van Diepen

The Devil's Eggs Are Hatching

Beads used:
11° Miyuki Delicas:

21
31V
34V
38
206
254 cut
502
732
851

11° Toho rounds:

D 485
PF 558

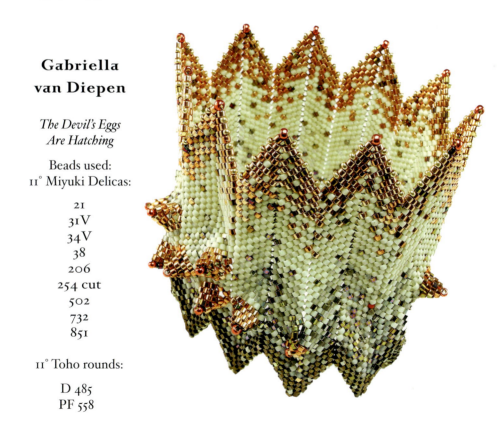

"In art as in love, instinct is enough."
Anatole France

Horned Rick-Rack

Gabriella van Diepen

Beads used:
11° Miyuki Delicas, including:

31
69
191
323
340
464
1012
1054

11° Toho rounds:
319
634B

15° Toho rounds:
457E

Gabriella calls this piece *Big Dipper,* and it reminds us of a starry night sky as seen from an ancient wood. Jeroen's wonderful close-up shots show that you can create Horns anywhere you can place a herringbone increase (which is almost anywhere you can place a single bead). *Photographs by Jeroen Medema.*

Maria Cristina Grifone

photo by Francesca Pavoni

Beads used:
11° Miyuki Delicas:

>   10
>   22
>   22L
>   31
>   35
>   630

"The most beautiful things in the world cannot be seen or touched, they are felt with the heart."

Antoine de Saint-Exupéry

In this piece we see every colour of the night sky; the pinkish gold of city lights to the hard white glitter of a thousand stars in perfect darkness.

Even the gleam of purple light just before dark is represented.

Horned Rick-Rack

For your first Horned Rick-Rack, you might wish to place your increases on the herringbone rows, as Maria Cristina Grifone did in these spectacular versions. Placing the horns on these "seams" is a bit easier to hold during increases, as the expansion of the wings matches the motion of the piece.

Maria Cristina's pieces remind us of circles of mountains, lakes, trees, and of silent woods and forests. The Rick-Rack lends itself very well to this sort of landscape painting in beads.

Maria Cristina Grifone

photo by Francesca Pavoni

Beads used:
11° Miyuki Delicas:

2 cut
27
40
44
147
608
1207

"Inspiration is needed in geometry, just as much as in poetry."

Aleksandr Pushkin

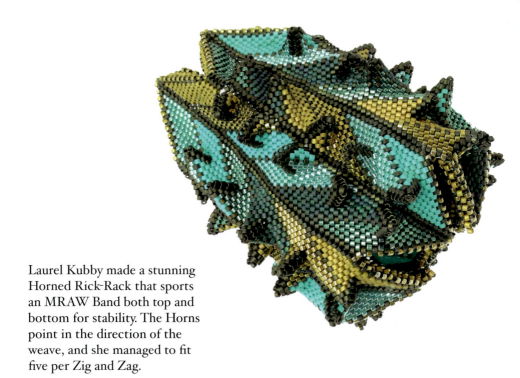

Laurel Kubby made a stunning Horned Rick-Rack that sports an MRAW Band both top and bottom for stability. The Horns point in the direction of the weave, and she managed to fit five per Zig and Zag.

Laurel Kubby

Beads used:
11° Miyuki Delicas:

238
311
327
371
456
458
759

"A great building must begin with the unmeasurable, must go through measurable means when it is being designed and in the end must be once again unmeasurable."

Louis Kahn

Contemporary Geometric Beadwork by Kate McKinnon 155

Zigged Parrot Tulips

Zigged Tulips and **Flowerbands** can be embellished differently on each side, and then joined at alternating points to create different flower shapes.

This tulip is completely different joined on one side or the other. The two photos on the left show one set of points drawn together, the two on the right connected with the alternate set. Try it both ways, and change the number of petals, adds, increases and decreases for new shapes.

"To me, a building, if it's beautiful, is the love of one man; he's made it out of his love for space, materials…"

Martha Graham

156   Contemporary Geometric Beadwork by Kate McKinnon

Materials: medium weight beading thread (we used Nymo B)
40-50 g. of 11° cylinder beads

Technique: All-Increase MRAW Bellyband, circular peyote

Tension: snug

Difficulty: Intermediate. Start with Rick-Rack.

The Zigged Band can make fabulous flowers as well as Rick-Rack, and can be built with all increases as well as alternating increases and decreases. This pretty five-petaled Parrot Tulip is a snap to create with a simple Band start.

We'll step this one all of the way out, but by all means experiment with the math to make a variety of shapes, points, and edges. If you would like six petals, place twelve increases, etc.

All-Increase MRAW Bellyband

To begin, bead an MRAW Bellyband, with the spacer every 10th gap being a 2-bead increase, for a total of 10 sets of increases.

If you look closely at the photographs, you can see double-horns at each petal tip. Those two horn shapes are the increases. Ten increases make five petals.

Use the final unit to close the band into a circle, and remember that unit is a part of your total count. If you want your petals to be even you must have your total units evenly divisible by your number of petals. Flowers in nature tend to be quite orderly, but happily you have no such obligation.

Zigged Parrot Tulips

Green Side (interior)

Round 1 – Peyote using light pink and continue the increases in every tenth space.

Round 2 – Peyote in dark green, creating a Point Round. Place a 15° between the beads at the "top" of the peaks as shown. Begin decreasing at the valleys; pass through the final light pink bead on the side, add a 15° and pass back through the first light pink bead of the next side.

Round 3 – Peyote using dark green. At the peaks pull the last and first dark green beads together to make a decrease. At the valleys, repeat, but also place a 15° between the two dark green beads.

Round 4 – Peyote using medium green. Each time you begin a new side, pull the existing green beads into a decrease. Again, and for the final time, place a 15° bead between the two dark green beads in the valley.

Round 5 – Peyote using light green, decreasing at every peak and valley.

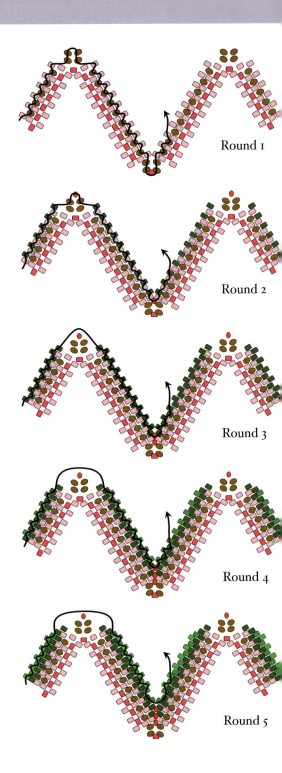

Round 1

Round 2

Round 3

Round 4

Round 5

158   Contemporary Geometric Beadwork by Kate McKinnon

Round 6 – Peyote using light green, decreasing at every peak and skipping through every valley. (Leaving these gaps was Kate's choice in creating her flower; feel free to make your own decisions about gaps or decreases)

Round 7 - Peyote using light green, decreasing only in the peaks and skipping through the valleys. Needle through the beadwork to arrive at the location to resume beading.

Round 8 – Peyote using light blue, decreasing only at the peaks and needling through your work in the valleys.

Round 9 – Peyote in light blue. Continue as you like to completely close your flower, or leave gaps. Kate left the gaps that she did so that the flower would close enough to resemble a Parrot Tulip.

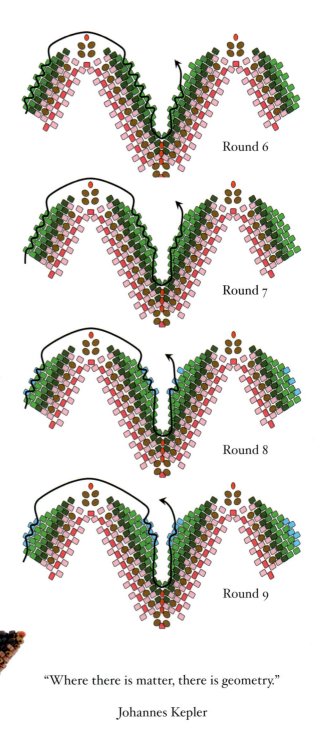

Round 6

Round 7

Round 8

Round 9

"Where there is matter, there is geometry."

Johannes Kepler

Zigged Parrot Tulips

Pink Side (petals)

Round 1: Place the 11° round spacer beads. Every 10th bead should be alternately an increase (2 beads) or decrease (0 beads).

Round 2: Peyote using light pink, continuing the increases and decreases as established.

Round 3: Peyote using dark pink, continuing the increases and decreases.

Round 4: Peyote using light pink, continuing the increases and decreases.

Round 5: Peyote using dark pink, continuing the increases and decreases.

Join the petals on either end to create two different tulip shapes.

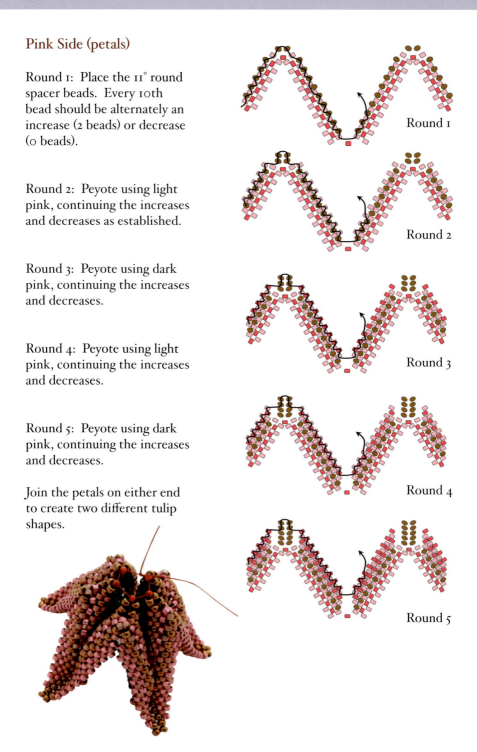

160   Contemporary Geometric Beadwork by Kate McKinnon

In the flower below, the Band is built of 11° cranberry Delicas and spaced with 11° bronze rounds. There is a hot pink peyote round on each side of the spacers, and a 4-round decrease at the top. The band is then connected in the center, and ornamented with hot red 13° rounds.

Make a wide variety of flower forms by changing the placement of the increases and decreases in an MRAW Bellyband.

Above: an MRAW flower in four shades of bronze with a center bezel, by the mighty Rayo Boursier. She says, "This was a natural evolution. It started out as a Rick-Rack bangle but was a little too tight for my wrists so I put it down on my bead board and there it was! A flower!"

Below: Kate likes to connect her flowers into necklaces using beaded strips to join the flowers to each other, or, better yet, to forged metal rings.

"The meaning of things lies not in the things themselves, but in our attitude towards them."

Antoine de Saint-Exupéry

Contemporary Geometric Beadwork by Kate McKinnon

Right: beady flowers make fabulous rings. Kate made a nifty MRAW ring shank for this one, adding a few rows of peyote and finishing the edges with the same bronze 11° rounds that she put in the middle of the Bellyband.

Above and right: the Band for a 2-3" Zigged Flower is generally bracelet-sized, and makes a lovely little bangle.

Simply push it flat onto the table to see how it can form a flower. Beadwork, this page, by Kate McKinnon.

See more flowers and Zigged Delights in our companion eBook (we simply couldn't stuff them all into the paper version) and watch for new updates and beady patterns and mobile Apps from the entire Team on the CGB Book Blog.

Find links at www.katemckinnon.com
and www.ContemporaryGeometricBeadwork.com

Our lovely Fortuneteller pattern, shown in the following pages of **Glorious Combinations**, is an elegant combination of Rick-Rack and Wings and Horns, and is another very flower-inspired use of a Zigged Band. The piece above is in progress, and was beaded by JoAnn Baumann.

Good bones are so important. As Frank Lloyd Wright says,

"A doctor can bury his mistakes, but an architect can only advise his clients to plant vines."

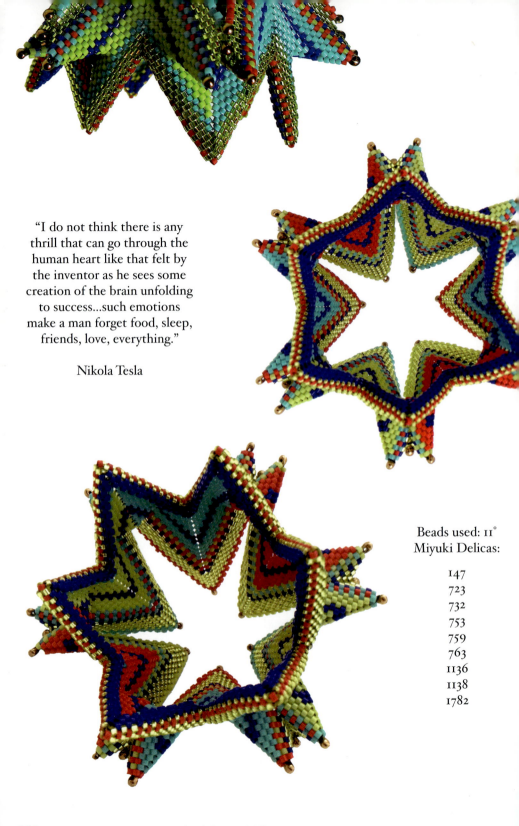

"I do not think there is any thrill that can go through the human heart like that felt by the inventor as he sees some creation of the brain unfolding to success...such emotions make a man forget food, sleep, friends, love, everything."

Nikola Tesla

Beads used: 11° Miyuki Delicas:

147
723
732
753
759
763
1136
1138
1782

Glorious Combinations:
Fortuneteller Bangle

This exquisite piece was designed by Christina Vandervlist, a product of the heady brew of her own inquisitive nature, the clever Zigged Band dreamed up by Dustin Wedekind and Kate McKinnon, and the Horned Rick-Rack Bangle.

This sturdy architecture of Zigs and folds was sauced with the soars and swoops of Wings and Horns, and ended up reminding us of the little origami paper forms we would fold as children. We called them whirlybirds or cootie-catchers or fortunetellers, and they told us who we would marry and how many babies we would have. (Or who would kiss us and how many times, depending on who did the folding.)

This piece was greatly loved by the crack team of Irregulars who were beading up a storm during the creation of this book. Their exquisite variations are presented with bead colour numbers, and Christina's basic pattern may be found beginning on pg. 188.

"The essence of all beautiful art, all great art, is gratitude."

Friedrich Nietzsche

Christina Vandervlist

Beads used: 11° Miyuki Delicas:

159	727
246	1340
262	1371
722	1573

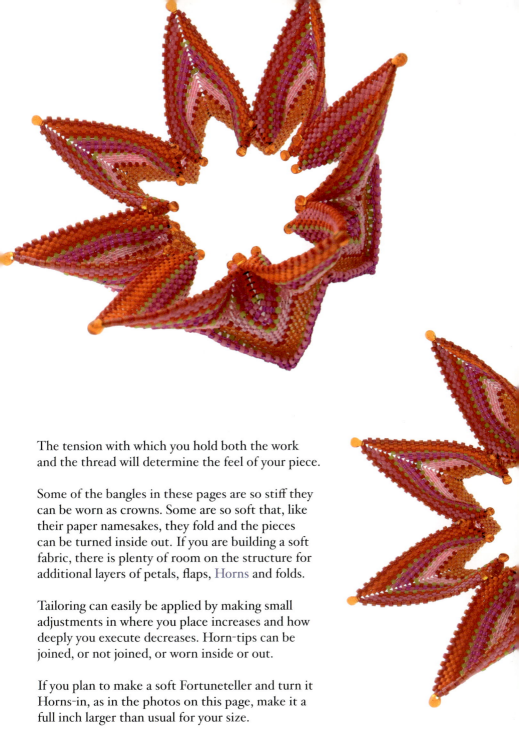

The tension with which you hold both the work and the thread will determine the feel of your piece.

Some of the bangles in these pages are so stiff they can be worn as crowns. Some are so soft that, like their paper namesakes, they fold and the pieces can be turned inside out. If you are building a soft fabric, there is plenty of room on the structure for additional layers of petals, flaps, Horns and folds.

Tailoring can easily be applied by making small adjustments in where you place increases and how deeply you execute decreases. Horn-tips can be joined, or not joined, or worn inside or out.

If you plan to make a soft Fortuneteller and turn it Horns-in, as in the photos on this page, make it a full inch larger than usual for your size.

Laurel Kubby

Beads used: 11° Miyuki Delicas:

11
124
133
311
391

and 3mm gold luster green tea Magatama drops
457

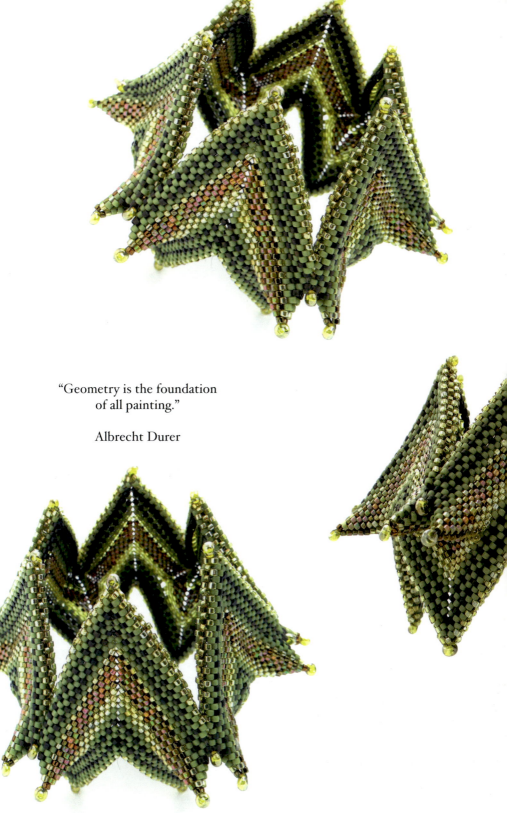

"Geometry is the foundation of all painting."

Albrecht Durer

Contemporary Geometric Beadwork by Kate McKinnon

"The artist is a receptacle for emotions that come from all over the place: from the sky, from the earth, from a scrap of paper, from a passing shape, from a spider's web."

Pablo Picasso

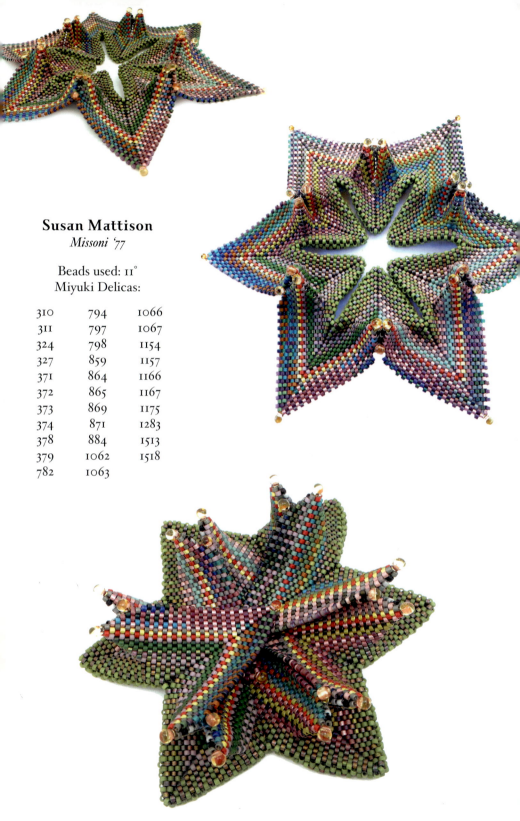

Susan Mattison
Missoni '77

Beads used: 11° Miyuki Delicas:

310	794	1066
311	797	1067
324	798	1154
327	859	1157
371	864	1166
372	865	1167
373	869	1175
374	871	1283
378	884	1513
379	1062	1518
782	1063	

Rayo Boursier

Beads used: 11°
Miyuki Delicas:
> 230
> 310
> 327
> 378

and: 11°
Toho Aikos:
> 10 F
> 123
> AK 222 T

and: 11°
Toho Treasures:
> 11-221
> (Bellyband)

"I found I could say things with color and shapes that I couldn't say any other way; things I had no words for."

Georgia O'Keeffe

Contemporary Geometric Beadwork by Kate McKinnon   173

"...the hand can never execute anything higher than the heart can imagine."

Ralph Waldo Emerson

Contemporary Geometric Beadwork by Kate McKinnon

Kat Oliva

Beads used: 11°
Miyuki Delicas:

> 322
> 371
> 653
> 671
> 795
> 1054
> 1055
> 1684
> 1768

Contemporary Geometric Beadwork by Kate McKinnon   175

"Breathe-in experience, breathe-out poetry."

Muriel Rukeyser

JoAnn Baumann

Beads used: 11°
Miyuki Delicas:
10
658
660
723
733

Eileen Montgomery

Beads used: 11° Miyuki Delicas:

116
177
707
725
798
1746

"Looking out into the universe at night, we make no comparisons between right and wrong stars, nor between well and badly arranged constellations."

Alan Watts

Contemporary Geometric Beadwork by Kate McKinnon   179

"Everything one invents is true, you may be perfectly sure of that. Poetry is as precise as geometry."

Gustave Flaubert

Julie Glasser

Beads used: 11° Miyuki Delicas:

10
29
323
380
1053

Christina Porter

Beads used: 11°
Miyuki Delicas:

6
58
311
862

15° Toho rounds:
167 BDF

Edging your beadwork makes not only for a clean finish but for longer wear, and if you use a fresh thread to do it, you give your finished bangle a huge advantage.

Christina Porter chose iridescent green charlotte-cut 11° rounds for her outer edge, and tiny 15° rounds for a neat picot on her inner edge.

Edging is a nice spot to use threads that you love but that are impractical for precision construction, such as silks, floss, and fine ribbon. Edges are also perfect for coloured Nymo or Silamide, if you like the look of fiber but prefer another type of thread for your beadweaving.

"The stars are the apexes of what triangles!"

Henry David Thoreau

Gabriella van Diepen

Beads used: 11°
Miyuki Delicas:

165
609
1011
1012
1054
1062

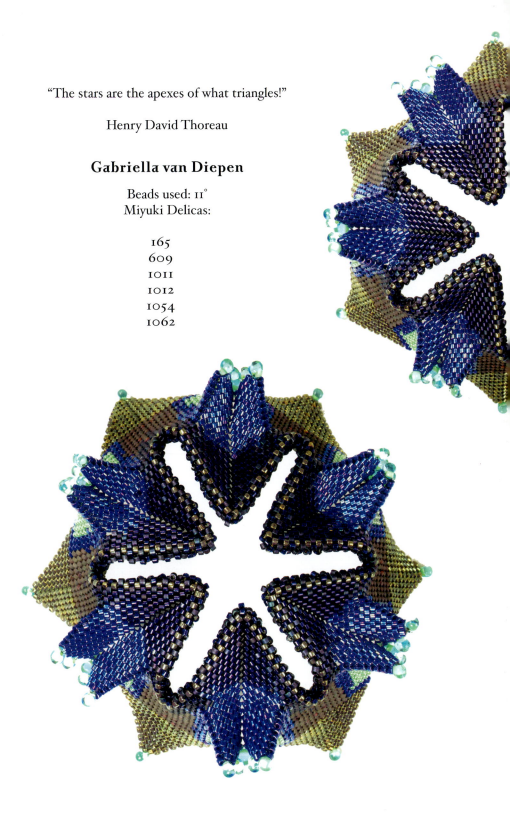

Julie Glasser

Beads used: 11° Miyuki Delicas:

335
1153
1155
1156
1157
1158
1159
1181

"I have stretched ropes from steeple to steeple; garlands from window to window; golden chains from star to star, and I dance."

Arthur Rimbaud

Julie built her Fortuneteller flat, which is an exciting way to realize the pattern. Each petal flexes with the orientation of this piece, for a different look in every incarnation. There are several snap-on elements, allowing the piece to be worn as a bracelet, a choker, or a collarbone-length necklace.

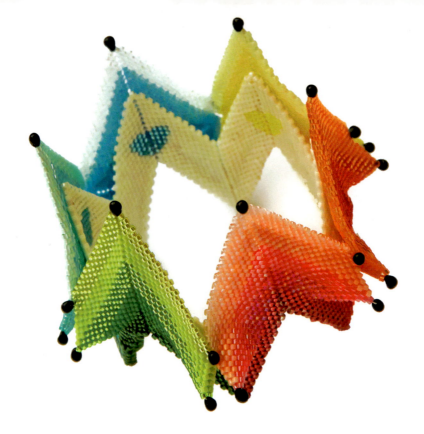

"Some painters transform the sun
into a yellow spot,
others transform a yellow spot
into the sun."

Pablo Picasso

Maria Cristina made this double-layered piece to mimic the white paper and coloured pencil versions we used to fold as children.

The inside figures, which look a bit like dots in this photograph (and inspired the Picasso quote) are actually little beady hearts, again calling to mind the theme of our love-inspired paper foldies from long ago.

Maria Cristina Grifone

photograph by Francesca Pavoni

Beads used: 11° Miyuki Delicas:

43	149	274
45	151	428
53	160	607
57	169	626
75	182	651
79	203	722
83	207	1132
85	232	1133
106	236	1206
147	238	1208
		1209

Miyuki Drops: 3.4 mm, black

Gabriella van Diepen modeling her Fortuneteller Bangle.
Photo by Jeroen Medema.

Fortuneteller Bangle

Materials:	medium to heavyweight beading thread (we used Nymo B & D) 40-50 g. of 11° cylinder beads
Technique:	Zigged MRAW Band, Rick-Rack, Wings, Horns, square stitch
Tension:	moderate to snug, as desired
Difficulty:	Advanced: start with both Rick-Rack and a Horned Bangle

There is a lot of room for innovation in this excellent design from Christina Vandervlist. We recommend that you read the whole pattern before you begin; you've got options, some of which are best planned for in advance.

The RAW band is architecture that is available to you at all times. The mighty Band can support one or more additional layers, and those layers can be directed up, down, or outward. It would be quite simple to add a third layer to Maria Cristina's double-layered piece (pg. 186) just by starting another peyote layer from the underside of the Band, or by placing a Guide Round at any point.

Even a four-layer Fortuneteller could easily be created with a single or a double Zigged Band (see the Triple Crown Rick-Rack Bangle, pg. 41). Your Winging, Horning, and layering are only restricted by what can fit into physical space, and the level of magnificence you are willing to wear.

Plan Your Size / MRAW Zigged Band

Each starting Peak for the Fortuneteller has 22 RAW units; 11 per Peak side. The increases and decreases alternate in every 11th slot in the line of spacers. (Zigged Bands have their Zigs and Zags set directly into the MRAW. See the illustration below.)

Small:	Six sets of Wings	(22 x 6 = 132 units)
Medium:	Seven sets of Wings	(22 x 7 = 154 units)
Large:	Eight sets of Wings	(22 x 8 = 176 units)

Remember to count the joining unit in the total. Make the Zigged Band nice and tight, and join it smoothly and securely. It should hold form from the very first round.

Inner Layer

Before you build a cathedral on one side of the Band, reinforce the other. A good foundation for building makes every step easier, including holding the work.

The Fortuneteller begins just like a double-layer Rick-Rack Bangle (see pg. 140). Needle to the side of the Band without MRAW spacers, and add at least six rounds of peyote Rick-Rack, following the pattern built into the band of increases and decreases in each 11th space. Christina's vivid Fortuneteller (below) uses cobalt beads for this short little layer.

If you plan to add a full inner sleeve of Rick-Rack, you can build that entire layer now, or alternate adding to inner and outer layers as the work grows. Either way, get a few rounds onto the inside as a first step, to stabilize the start. If you wish to stop the inner layer after just a few rounds, finish the inner edge before moving on. Trying to go back to the inner layer and bead it later only works if the piece is very soft and flexible.

If you'd like a Guide Round in the Band for a third layer of Peaks, place it while you still have easy access to the Band. Our samples do not show secondary structures, or mirror-Fortunetellers with Wings and Peaks on both sides of the Band, or Triple-Horned Winged Whirlybirds, but that's *only* because we stopped beading to write this book.

Christina's original Fortuneteller bangle has an excitingly cobalt inner layer.

Fortuneteller Bangle

Figs. 1 and 2 show the Zigged Band with and without the thread path. Amazingly, this is just one round of beadwork; the increases and decreases are placed when the MRAW Bellyband is built.

Fig. 3 shows the Band with six completed rounds of an inner layer.

Below: Susan Mattison's inner layer is a significant design feature, despite being small in size and worked in a low-key moss green. Imagine it in different colours...different beads, different sizes...see in your mind how changing that section changes the piece.

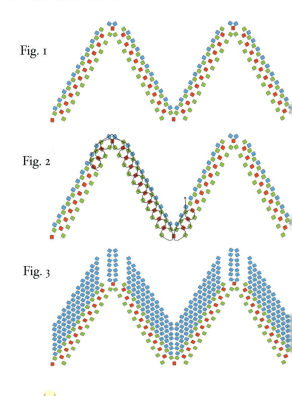

Fig. 1

Fig. 2

Fig. 3

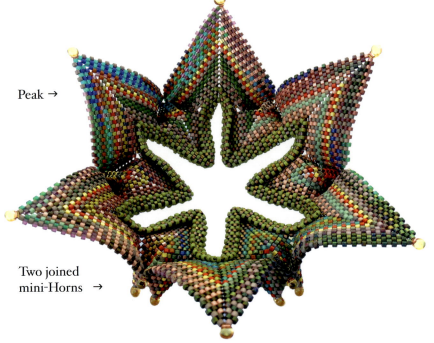

Peak →

Two joined mini-Horns →

190 Contemporary Geometric Beadwork by Kate McKinnon

Outer Layers

Needle out to the other side of the Zigged Band (with the MRAW spacers).

Mirroring the placement of Band increases and decreases, peyote six rounds of Rick-Rack. In Fig. 4, we have 7 rounds placed. (Be thinking about the math here; we're simply reporting what we did to make this shape. So much else is possible. When you change the numbers, you change the shape.)

In the next round, place two-bead increases in the center spaces of each side of each Peak (see Fig. 5). Be careful to continue *all* increases, those at the tops of each Peak and those on the little mini-Horns growing in the sides of each Peak. Continue for a total of 8 rounds.

The piece will feel very sprawly in your hands.

Peyote another round, placing normal increases at the top of each Peak, but instead of continuing to increase at the mini-Horns, place a mini-drop at the tip of each one. The mini-drops on the mini-Horns are a Point Round; the mini-Horn increases are complete.

If your tension is snug, you should begin to see the shape firming up now.

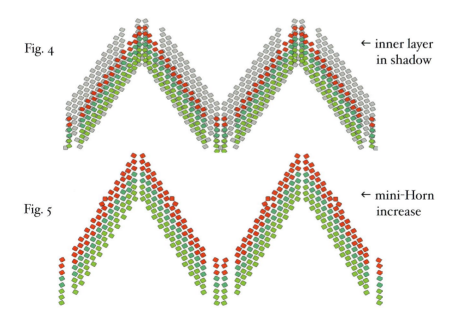

Fig. 4 ← inner layer in shadow

Fig. 5 ← mini-Horn increase

Contemporary Geometric Beadwork by Kate McKinnon

Fortuneteller Bangle

Decreasing the Mini-Horns

Peyote 7 rounds, decreasing the mini-Horns while continuing to grow the main Peaks. After these 7 rounds, the mini-Horn decreases will have paired up at the side of each section, and you will be able to see the structure of your work. (Things will get a lot easier to hold as well.)

Peyote another round. In this round, each time you come to the section between the main Peaks where the mini-Horns have connected, pass through the existing beads and square stitch them together to reinforce the connection (see illustration, opposite page).

Place an ornamental mini-drop at the join, if you like, after square stitching and before continuing on with the peyote. You see this drop bead in the photo below, just under the two drops at the tip of each mini-Horn.

Peyote a final round. Place a mini-drop in place of each main Peak decrease (this is the bottom drop in the cluster of four in the photo below) and instead of an increase at the tip of each Peak, place another mini-drop. See these at the bottoms of the main peaks, also below.

That's where we stopped our pattern. We can't wait to see what you make.

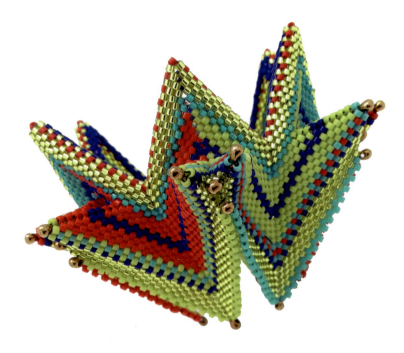

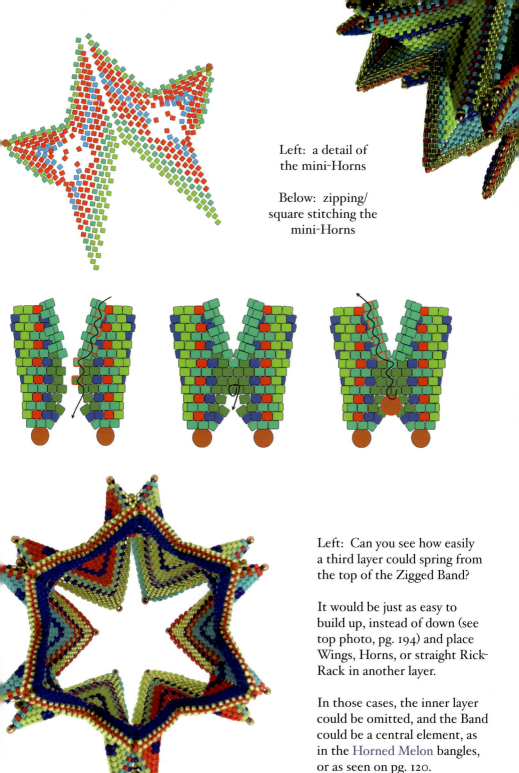

Left: a detail of the mini-Horns

Below: zipping/square stitching the mini-Horns

Left: Can you see how easily a third layer could spring from the top of the Zigged Band?

It would be just as easy to build up, instead of down (see top photo, pg. 194) and place Wings, Horns, or straight Rick-Rack in another layer.

In those cases, the inner layer could be omitted, and the Band could be a central element, as in the Horned Melon bangles, or as seen on pg. 120.

Contemporary Geometric Beadwork by Kate McKinnon   193

Left: The Fortuneteller just after the addition of the mini-drops, and just before the mini-Horn decrease begins.

Left: A nice end view of the four mini-drops on the mini-Horn tips, the join of the decreases, and the crotch of the two Peaks.

"Begin at the beginning and go on till you come to the end: then stop."

Lewis Carroll,
Alice in Wonderland

"You can always add more later, because you built it on a Band!"

Us

"Nine-tenths of tactics are certain, and taught in books: but the irrational tenth is like the kingfisher flashing across the pool..."

T.E. Lawrence

Above: The colourway of Eileen Montgomery's piece is perfect for studying the structures of the increases (light turquoise) and decreases (dark turquoise) and how they relate to the Peaks and Horns. See more of this piece on pgs. 178-179.

Left: Christina's pink bangle, on the other hand, emphasizes a seamless horizontal flow.

Contemporary Geometric Beadwork by Kate McKinnon

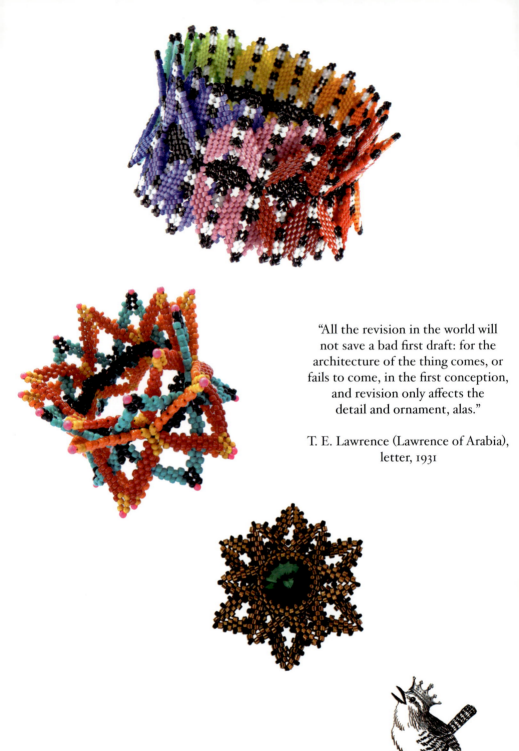

"All the revision in the world will not save a bad first draft: for the architecture of the thing comes, or fails to come, in the first conception, and revision only affects the detail and ornament, alas."

T. E. Lawrence (Lawrence of Arabia), letter, 1931

196   Contemporary Geometric Beadwork by Kate McKinnon

Helix Bangle

The Helix pattern was inspired by the open-add technique that Jean Power used to make her Rivoli Star (opposite). During a few days of play with the technique, Christina made an exciting sketch of a Helixy idea in bright 8° round beads. The lush Rainbow Triple Helix Bangle in 11° cylinder beads followed rapidly.

In this section, we present both the original pattern and a host of delightful variations made by beaders worldwide.

Above: Helix strap bracelet by Deb Bednarek
Opposite page, top: Rainbow Triple Helix by Christina Vandervlist
Opposite page, middle: Helix Sketch in 8° Rounds by Christina Vandervlist
Opposite page, bottom: the inspiration: a Rivoli Star by Jean Power

Shelley Gross

Beads used: Silverlined 11° Miyuki Delicas:

47	1201
150	1202
182	1341
607	1345
608	1681

"The sound of colours is so definite that it would be hard to find anyone who would express bright yellow with bass notes or dark lake with treble..."

Wassily Kandinsky

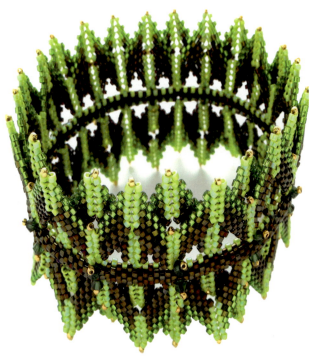

Beatrice Childress
Artichoke Helix

Beads used: A dusting of 24k 15° rounds and 11° Miyuki Delicas:

11
169
182
311

Beatrice added extra rows of peyote to cover her Bellyband with a bit of tube. Her bangle reminds us, delightfully, of a ring of trees reflected in a lake.

Julie Glasser

Beads used:
11° Miyuki Delicas:

321	878
335	879
336	1153
371	1154
374	1158
376	1164
758	1172
760	1173
867	

"A poem is never finished, only abandoned."

Paul Valéry

Julie's tension is very soft in comparison to most of our beaders. Her pieces make neat little rolls, they fold up in the palm of your hand. They are as soft as a whisper to wear. Either you work this way or you don't; Kate McKinnon has a similarly soft hand, whereas Christina Vandervlist, when learning to bead crochet, made a rod. A crocheted rod.

Seeing the many different versions of our pieces come in was very informative. We found that both soft and stiff versions of the work were equally appealing; each approach has advantages. The only generalization that we feel that we can make about tension is that whether you work tightly or softly, what you don't want to do is work loosely. Keep it snug.

Deb Bednarek

Beads used: Swarovski copper crystal accents and 11° Miyuki Delicas:

21	321
21/ L	334
22/ cut	457
23	512
34	513
126	

Deb chose to build her Helix as a strap band, and fastened it both with a button and loop and with a hidden snap. This is elegant tailoring for a strap closure; it prevents sagging.

Karin Salomon

Beads used: Czech rounds:

Picasso Green
Picasso Yellow
Clear-Lined Gold
Silver-lined Frosted Topaz

Karin's painterly colourway shows the spare elegance of Christina's Helix Sketch pattern (see pg. 209) well.

200   Contemporary Geometric Beadwork by Kate McKinnon

Karin Salomon
Monet's Garden

Beads used: 11° Miyuki Delicas from a mix called "Field Of France", including:

102
174
864
877
881

Karin used a mix of matte and transparent beads, to add dimension and depth to her colours. (It worked.)

She also overlapped her Helix Points. To do this, feed new Point adds through the legs of their neighbors.

Nancy Hepp

Beads used: 11° Miyuki Delicas:

34
203
310

Nancy's swank Tuxedo Helix looks black and white, but her white is actually a pale lustre yellow, DB 203.

Contemporary Geometric Beadwork by Kate McKinnon

Triple Helix Bangle

The Helix pattern uses an open-add technique to place overlapping layers of Helix Points on the edges and center of a double-wide Modified RAW Bellyband. Join the band into a bangle or make it strap-style, with a closure.

The Points are built to the desired height using Peyote Zig-Zag stitch. Like our Rick-Rack Bangle, the Helix rises higher by adding two beads at the top of each Point (the increase) and passing through the two crotch beads at the base of each leg without adding any beads (the decrease).

Christina placed a total of six separate overlapping rounds of Points; two above and two below the Bellyband, and the final two anchored in the center line of the Band beads.

Materials: medium to heavy beading thread (we used Nymo B & D) approx. 36 g. of 11°cylinder beads (3 g. each of 12 colours)

Technique: MRAW Bellyband, open-add peyote start, Rick-Rack stitch

Tension: very snug

Difficulty: Intermediate. Start with Rick-Rack and the Power Puff Bangle.

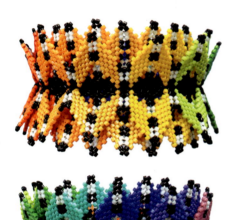

Our sample uses 11° Miyuki Delicas (listed in order of appearance):

(A1)	10	Black
(A2)	200	White
(B1)	723	Red
(B2)	722	Vivid Orange
(B3)	1133	Light Orange
(B4)	651	Goldenrod
(B5)	1132	Yellow
(B6)	733	Lime Green
(B7)	724	Green
(B8)	1136	Turq. Blue
(B9)	1138	Blue
(B10)	661	Violet
(B11)	1376	Berry
(B12)	654	Maroon

Christina chose glossy black for both her Bellyband and its spacers, which is beautiful but hard to count. In the following pages, we've illustrated it with the spacer rows in blue and the RAW beads in green so you can see the thread path. Unless you are an old hand with MRAW, we recommend using a contrasting colour for the spacer row.

Triple Helix Bangle

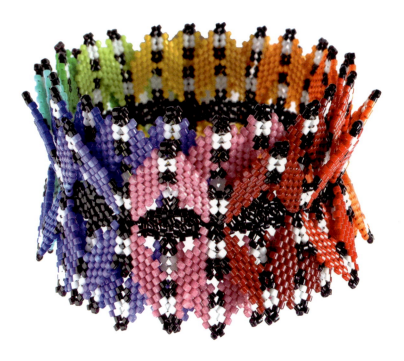

1. **Double MRAW Bellyband** (see pg. 39 for MRAW tutorial)

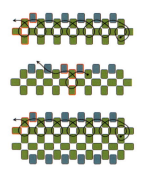

Make a snug, even Double MRAW Bellyband. (Consistency with the thread path is important.)

Join the Bellyband if you are making a bangle, or work it flat if you are making a strip bracelet. Please refer to the sizing discussion on the opposite page to decide your band length.

Reinforce the band edges with an additional pass of thread, if necessary.

2. Sizing

The Helix can be made as a bangle, in which case you would join the Bellyband before adding Points (so that the Points can overlap the join for a seamless Helix) or flat, to finish with a closure.

Our bangle-style sample is made for a medium hand with a total of 84 RAW units. (It's easiest to count the spacers, which also handily number 84, and this is why it's easiest to choose a different colour for those beads.) Obviously a strap band, which must only fit the wrist, can be made smaller.

Each Point set covers 8 RAW units, which is a large increment in bracelet sizing. To remove one set of Points to fit a very small hand, you will have to drop a colour, and eliminate 7 RAW units from the band, for a total of 77. (Why do we say that each Point covers 8 units, but to remove one we only take out 7 units? Because each Point shares an attachment bead with its neighbor.)

To make a larger bangle, add another set of Points (seven RAW units) for an MRAW band size of 91 units. If your measurements fall in an awkward spot for sizing this piece as a bangle, or if you are just learning the Helix, it might work out better for you as a flat strip.

The Helix, assuming you are working it tightly, should not shrink more than 1/4" when the second row is added and the Points go on. If your Bellyband is not tight and firm, reinforce or redo it before you begin the Helix, as the band supports the entire piece.

Before you join the Bellyband, be sure that it goes over your hand with a tiny bit of room to spare. A bangle sizer (left) is invaluable for helping calculate bangle closures. See Sizing, pg. 26.

Triple Helix Bangle

Fig. 1

3. Adding Helix Points

Needle out so that you are exiting an outside edge bead of the MRAW band (not the spacer beads – they're for the next set of Points).

String 22 beads in the first colour and pass through the outside edge bead of the seventh unit along (Fig. 1).

For our 84-unit band, we repeated this add x 11 to complete a total of twelve Points, and we met our first Point at the base of our last. (Your sizing may dictate a different number of Points, or space between them.)

In our sample, there are 12 beads per Point. (A) is the colour of the base band, and (B) is the colour of the Point. String 1(A), 9(B), 2(A), 9(B) and 1(A). The (B) bead will change colour with each Point.

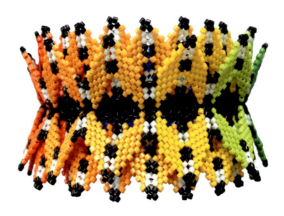

4. Adding Peyote to the Points

Fig. 2

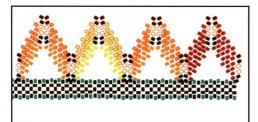

Fig. 3

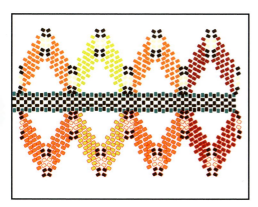

Fig. 4

Peyote stitch 5 single beads, 1 into each of the 5 spaces that climb the first leg, using 1(A), 4(B).

Place 2(A) beads atop the two beads at the top of the Point, then peyote stitch the next 5 spaces using 4(B) and 1(A).

Pass through the two crotch beads at the base of the legs without adding beads. (Fig. 2)

In this way, using an increase of 2 beads at the top of each Point, and a pass-through decrease through the two beads at the bottoms of the legs, the Points grow taller.

Finish the round, using a new colour for each Point.

Repeat this round four times to make each Point six rounds high. (Fig. 3)

Weave down into the base Band and repeat the Points on the opposite side. (Fig. 4)

> To create the black and white checkerboard effect shown in our sample, alternate the (A) beads, using two rounds with (A1) (black), two rounds using (A2) (white), and then two more rows of (A1) (black).

Contemporary Geometric Beadwork by Kate McKinnon   207

Triple Helix Bangle

To add the second row of Points, weave down into the Bellyband and exit from the spacer bead in the center of a previously added Point. Previous rounds are now shown in shadow. (Fig. 5)

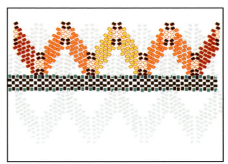

Fig. 5

To repeat our progression, use the same colours in the same order for this layer as in your first round. Alternately, vary each layer by tone or theme. (Fig. 6)

For the third and final layers, anchor the Points into the RAW beads in the center of the Bellyband. (Fig. 7)

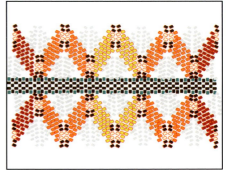

Fig. 6

Optional Tailoring

To keep the final layer of Points slightly elevated, instead of passing through the valleys, peyote into the decreases to add a single bead into the crotch. This will ensure that the outer row of Points stands out with a bit of attitude.

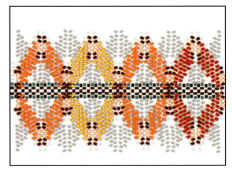

Fig. 7

"How often I found where I should be going only by setting out for somewhere else...most of my advances were by mistake. You uncover what is when you get rid of what isn't."

Buckminster Fuller

208   Contemporary Geometric Beadwork by Kate McKinnon

Materials:
Approx. 60 grams of 8° Japanese round beads.

Sturdy thread : we used Nymo D.

Christina used lovely gloss 8° beads in shades of orange, turquoise, black, red, yellow, and hot pink.

"Drawing is the honesty of the art. There is no possibility of cheating. It is either good or bad."

Salvador Dalí

Helix Sketch: Bangle in 8° Rounds

To fit a medium wrist and hand, begin with an MRAW Bellyband 55 units long. Five Points per round cover 11 units each, and each Point begins with 26 beads strung.

Adjust the length of the band start (and/or the width and number of Points per round) for size. Peyote only twice around each set of Points, and add a total of six rounds, three above and three below the Bellyband.

Due to the extra weight of the large 8° beads, only the Helix Points on the outermost rounds are anchored in the outside edge RAW units. The Points for rounds 3 through 6 all originate using the center beads of the Bellyband as their anchor. Because of this, you may want to reinforce your Bellyband with an extra pass of thread before beginning to add the Points.

See another version in 8° beads by Karin Salomon on pg. 200.

Above: *First Helix Sketch,* Christina Vandervlist

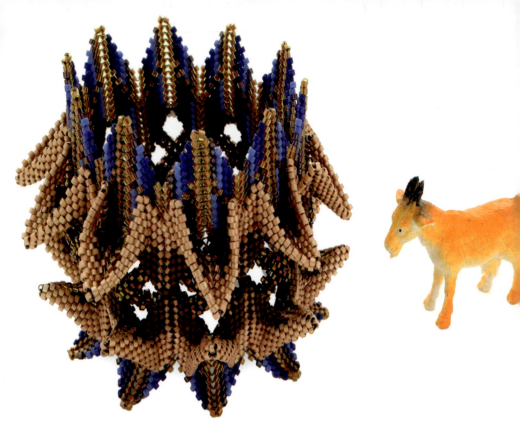

Not even a plastic goat could make a guess at what to call Rayo Boursier's extraordinary piece. Kate named it an *X-Wing*, but that's as close as anyone has come to defining it. In this single piece, Rayo captured every technique in this book except Cones, and went beyond us to create a 3-D X-Band. Perhaps the piece needs companion earrings with orange Cone-tips or a single, conical barnacle, or an ambassadorship to outer space.

All we know for certain is that for some reason we can't explain, it leaves us wanting to fly a fighter jet, or longing for the sea.

> "If you want to build a ship, don't drum up people together to collect wood and don't assign them tasks and work, but rather teach them to long for the endless immensity of the sea."
>
> Antoine de Saint-Exupéry

210   Contemporary Geometric Beadwork by Kate McKinnon

Rayo Boursier

X-Wing

Rayo has one very important piece of advice for anyone who is planning on making a 3-D X-Band out of 15° charlotte-cuts: "Don't." We have to laugh, though, because after seeing this piece, it's all we want to do.

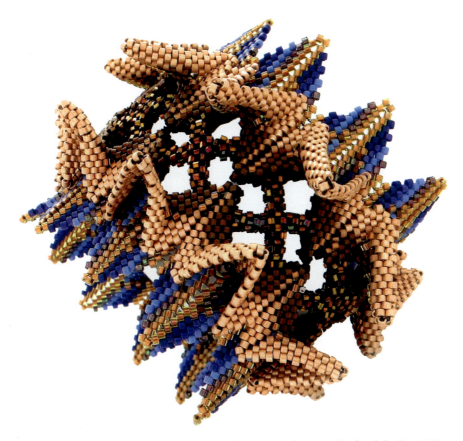

Kirsty Little
Helixed Rick-Rack

Beads used:
11° Miyuki Delicas:

73
79
169
253
1764

Helix Points can be placed on many different types of structures.

In this piece, Kirsty Little placed two rounds of them on the outside of a Rick-Rack Bangle. Anywhere you can securely anchor a set of single beads into a piece, you can start a Helix add.

A central Bellyband would make anchoring the open-add Points a bit easier, but Kirsty found that she had enough room in her peyote structure to squeeze them in. Think of the possibilities!

"Necessity may be the mother of invention, but
play is certainly the father."

Roger von Oech

Nancy Graver made an incredible Fortunetellerish flower cluster on the end of a *Ginkgo Leaves* lariat (a Diane Fitzgerald pattern) long before we dreamed up the Fortuneteller or the easy MRAW start for these structures.

Nancy sewed squares in peyote and zipped them together, but you can see how the shapes echo the increases and decreases of the all-in-one Fortuneteller Bangle. It's a beautiful (and beautifully made) piece.

Nancy Graver

Ginkgo Lariat with Flower Cluster Tips

Jalisco Bangle

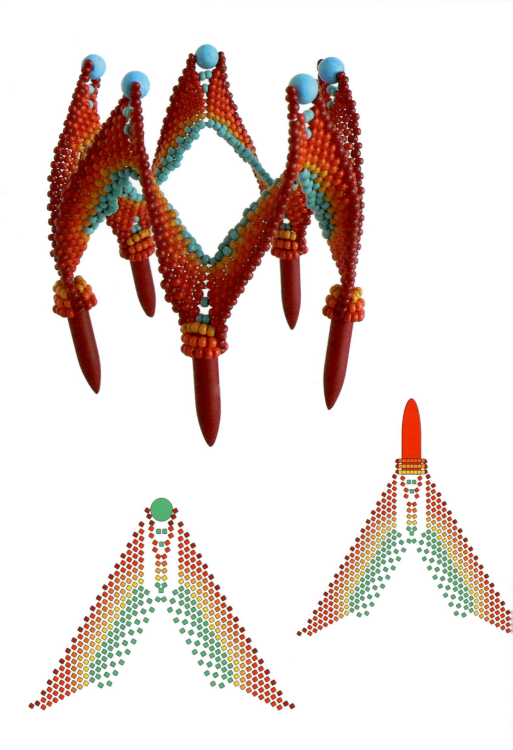

214 Contemporary Geometric Beadwork by Kate McKinnon

Cath Thomas made her fabulous Jalisco Bangle in 11° round seed beads before we began our own Winging or Bellybanding. She was pleased to incorporate our Band into her design, and made the Jalisco below out of cylinder beads using our MRAW start. These two bangles are a wonderful example of the different personalities of beads; the cylinders seem to freeze the piece in space, while the seed beads carry motion in their roundness, seeming to dance even while standing still.

We are fascinated by the way structures repeat themselves even in apparently unrelated pieces. For example, on the opposite page, in our illustrated details of the structure of Cath's points, can you see that the sections on either side of the points are just like Tri-Wing Rings?

We might not have noticed this family resemblance in the original seed bead piece, but when we diagrammed it, and of course when we saw the version done in cylinder beads, it was obvious. See our MRAW Flowers, another close cousin of Jalisco, on pgs. 161-162.

To create a Jalisco Bangle, make an MRAW Bellyband with 10 to 14 evenly spaced increases (fewer increases for smaller sizes). Keep your work tight if you want the bangle to stand. The points will alternate up and down of their own accord. When they are long enough, tip half of them with balls and half of them with daggers. Ornament the daggers with circles of beads to keep them erect.

Cath Thomas

Jalisco Bangles

photos by Cath Thomas

"Colours speak all languages."

Joseph Addison

Contemporary Geometric Beadwork by Kate McKinnon

Photo of Gabriella van Diepen by Kyle Cassidy

Cones

Gather up a little handful of round seed beads and prepare to be mesmerized by the spectacular Cone Stitch.

Single Cone by Dustin Wedekind
Cone Bangle by Jean Campbell

Contemporary Geometric Beadwork by Kate McKinnon

Basic Cone

This excellent spiral square stitch pattern developed by Dustin Wedekind and Christina Vandervlist can do much more than make a Cone, but Cones are a good place to start.

Begin yours by using square stitch to make a double-sided band. For the ruffled cone shown in the pattern, made by Christina, make one line (we'll call it a "round" for convenience) of beads in a solid colour and the other line in a repeating pattern of three beads and an accent bead.

Christina made this Cone into a flower brooch, using a sew-on finding.

Beads used, Basic Cone:

Czech round seed beads:
(A) 11° chartreuse
(B) 11° pink assortment
(C) 8° lustre white

Materials: medium to heavyweight beading thread (we used Nymo B and D) seed beads: 5 g. of 11° in two colours and 3 g. of 8° make a single Cone

Technique: spiral square stitch

Tension: moderate to snug

Difficulty: You can do it!

A – Solid colour 11°
B – Mixed colour 11°
C – Accent beads 8°

Make a Starting Coneladder

Step 1: Pick up 2 (A) and 2 (B) and join them into a tight little circle. Pass back through the 2 (A) beads.

Step 2: Pick up 1 (A) and 1 (B). Pass back through the previous (B) bead and back out the previous (A) and the new (A). You've just completed your first square stitch, and there are 3 (B) beads in a row.

Step 3: Pick up 1 (A) and 1 (C), and complete a square stitch (passing back into the previous B bead and then out the old *and* new A beads) to add these two new beads. This step introduces the first accent bead.

Step 1   Step 2   Step 3

Step 4: Continue adding beads, two at a time, using square stitch. One side of the growing ladder will stay all in one colour (A), while the other side will have a repeating pattern of 3 (B) then 1 (C).

Continue building this ladder until it is long enough to coil neatly over onto itself, in a diameter you can hold comfortably. We built this ladder to 25 units long before the overlapping join (please see the following page).

Bear in mind that it doesn't really matter where you join your Cone start. You can build in either direction, increasing or decreasing. We're just showing you the easiest way to hold it, which is to get a bit of ladder made before you overlap and join the ends.

Contemporary Geometric Beadwork by Kate McKinnon   219

Basic Cone

Step 5: Circle the ends around so that they overlap each other by the final three units just added. (Why three? Because it makes the smoothest join.)

Being careful to keep your work straight and untwisted, pass your needle back through the first three units of the start in reverse order, 3-2-1. Pass again through the final three units of the working end, as illustrated. Square stitch each pair together, to form a solid, yet flexible bond.

To make the join, overlap three units of the double strand (don't let them twist!) and square stitch them together. This is shown both in the round (below) and in each step of the pair connections (Figs. 1-3, right).

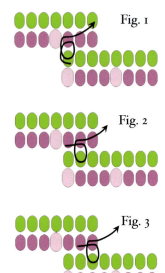

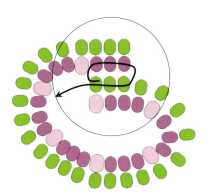

Step 6: Now that the spiral start is established, the Cone will grow by rounds of one bead, instead of the two you made at once while making your Coneladder start. Pick up 1 (B) or (C) bead (depending on where you are in your pattern) and square stitch it to the (A) bead directly below it.

Continue square stitching your way along the band, keeping to a pattern of adding 1 (C) after every series of 3 (B) beads.

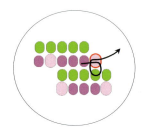

Illustrations in circles show only the area of the join.

Step 7:   Once you reach the "end of the line", you will be exiting into a space that is a row above the baseline. For your visualizing convenience, we drew this Step both in the round and also as a section.

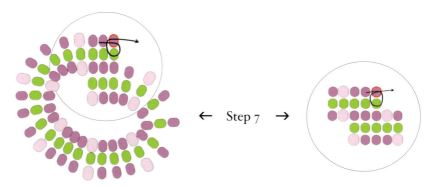

Step 8:   To get the needle to exit in the correct location to add another bead, pass back through the beads in a sensible path to exit in the lower row. Christina does it as drawn (right). This path passes through enough beads to hold securely, but doesn't pull the adjoining beads out of alignment.

It must be admitted that it doesn't really matter what you do first, because you can choose to go in either direction, increase or decrease, from your start. But for the sake of pattern-making, let's begin with the Flare (following page).

Contemporary Geometric Beadwork by Kate McKinnon

Basic Cone

Flaring The Cone

To flare this Cone, Christina took advantage of the visual cues given by the (C) beads to place her adds in the plain-colour round.

Step 9: To begin the increase, instead of adding a single (A) bead over each (C) bead, you will add two (A) beads. The band will feel a bit crowdy at first, and will look something like this, with the (A) beads rustling around on top of the patterned round.

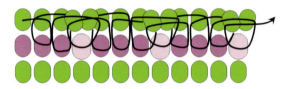

When you add the round of patterned beads above this expanded round, return to adding only a single bead for every bead in the row, using the same pattern, (B-B-B-C). In this manner, the diameter of the Cone increases gradually. Obviously, if you place more double-adds in Step 9, the Cone will flare more dramatically.

After the round of increase in the solid round, and the addition of a normal pattern round, the Cone structure looks like this:

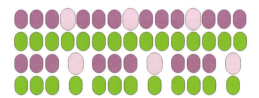

Finishing The Flared End of the Cone

Step 10: For a clean look, Christina finished her Cone with a round of (A) beads, and placed a little three-bead tuck on the exposed edge.

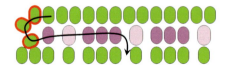

Decreasing The Cone

Step 11: Start a new thread, and/or needle down to the point at which you want to begin decreasing. Unlike the increases, which we placed in the plain round, our decreases are made in the patterned run of beads, which is simply the other side of our starting Coneladder.

To decrease the Cone, square stitch your (C) beads to two (A) beads instead of one. This is a nice, gradual decrease, and the pattern of (B-B-B-C) remains the same.

The decrease is shown below both in action, and in a flat pattern.

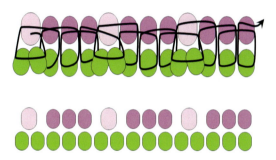

To finish a single Cone, decrease to the size point you want, and finish by weaving your thread in securely.

For a flower stem, decrease to the desired narrow diameter, and then simply continue the spiral, adding only one bead to one for as long as you like. Perhaps you'd like to make a Mobius DoubleCone, or a Cone Bangle, or a lusciously long lariat, like our Cones Of Darkness. See the following pages for a photo gallery of possibilities.

Obviously, this form has a great deal of room for play and innovation, and we plan to explore it more in Volume II of this book.

Right: a festive Cone by Dustin Wedekind.

Christina Vandervlist

Fabulous DoubleCone
Cocktail Ring

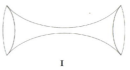

1. Make a DoubleCone of a suitable size to be a glamourous cocktail ring.

2. Slip it like a sock over a sturdy wire that has been bent into a ring that is just a *snitch* bigger than you need it to be.

3. Using round-nose pliers, finish the ends of the wire with a curl, trapping wired ornaments (right) or anything with a hole, or even another DoubleCone for a wild chain.

We use 16-12 gauge wire for this, depending on the metal, and how tight the beadwork is or isn't. A good all-purpose wire is 14 gauge sterling silver, half-hard.

"Poetry is when an emotion has found its thought and the thought has found words."

Robert Frost

Christina Vandervlist

Möbius DoubleCone Ring

Beads used:
Seed beads in 11° and 8°, in lavender, fuchsia, chartreuse and purple

Charlotte Aziz

DoubleCone Ring
with embellished felt balls

Beads used:
mixed Delica cylinders
and seed beads in 11° and 15°,
in turquoise, black, and silver

We love how the turquoise bead accents make it seem as if the felt continues through the ring as a band.
Photo by Charlotte.

Jean Campbell

Jean made an exciting, beautiful Many-Cone Bangle out of five Cones that grow out of a single tube. Her bangle closes with a magnetic clasp tucked inside and neatly bezeled with beads. Genius!

Beads used:
Seed beads in 11° and 8°, in black and silver

"A person often meets his destiny on the road he took to avoid it."

Jean de La Fontaine

Christina Vandervlist

Cones Of Darkness Lariat

Beads used:
Seed beads in 11° and 8°, in matte and shiny black

228 Contemporary Geometric Beadwork by Kate McKinnon

Left: Kate's Captain Kirk action figure (Yes! From the Gorn episode!) is holding several large Cones by Dustin Wedekind. *Photo by Bri Date.*

Below: Christina Vandervlist amazed us by whipping out a **TuTu Cuff** using the same spiral stitch. To make this, just make a Coneladder long enough to slip over your hand after the join. Add a few rounds without increase.

When you are ready to flare and ruffle, begin increasing, adding more and more two-bead increases until you have the look and the ruffle you want.

Thanks to

Barrel of Beads, Rhode Island
beadFX, Toronto, ON
Beads of Colour, Dundas, ON
Beyond Beadery, Colorado
www.DiMarca-Online.com
Eclectic, Devon, UK
Fire Mountain Gems
Glass Garden, Minnesota
Great Lakes Beadworkers Guild
Jean Power Beadwork
Out On A Whim, California
SeePerlen, Hanover, Germany
Spangles4Beads.co.uk
Tampa Bead Cafe, Florida
That Bead Lady, Newmarket, ON
Gail Crosman Moore

Everyone who pre-ordered!
We couldn't have done it without you!

Photography

Kate McKimmon
Kyle Cassidy
Jeroen Medema
Assorted Beaders (see page credits)

Illustration

Christina Vandervlist
Jean Power
Dustin Wedekind
Allison Shock

Invisible Friends

(Brush with lemon juice if names do not appear)

Bill McKinnon
Bryan Ferry
Miss Fish the cat
Dustin Wedekind
Buckminster Fuller
John Lautner
IPhone 4S camera
Isamu Noguchi
Ruth Asawa
Larry Gatti

Team Acknowledgements

Beaders Who Beaded (a-z)

Kelly Angeley
Charlotte Aziz
JoAnn Baumann
Deb Bednarek
Kim Boeckman
Rayo Boursier
Danielle M. Brown
Jean Campbell
Beatrice Childress
Jeannette Cook
Marcia DeCoster
Phyllis Dintenfass
Carla Engelman
Helen Fountain
Jenni Gerstle
Julie Glasser
Suzanne Golden
Nancy Graver
Mary Ruth Gray
Maria Cristina Grifone
Shelley Gross
Tiena Habing
Nancy Hepp
Cate Jones
Laurel Kubby

Alma Legacy
Barb Linkert
Kirsty Little
Jodie Marshall
Susan Mattison
Kate McKinnon
Jeroen Medema
Lia Melia
Eileen Montgomery
Kat Oliva
Christina Porter
Jean Power
A.J. Reardon
Ann Rishell
Karin Salomon
Teresa Sullivan
Carol Taylor
Cath Thomas
Christina Vandervlist
Gabriella van Diepen
Christina Vasil
Leslie Venturoso
Francesca Walton
Dustin Wedekind
Dana Steen Witker

The Mighty Edit Team

(without whom this book would be 50% less awesome)

Rayo Boursier
Beatrice Childress
Cynthia Fawcett
Nancy Graver
Doriot Lair
Eileen Montgomery
Kat Oliva
Lysa Schloesser
Cath Thomas
Francesca Watson
Sandy Wogaman

And don't miss these great books:
Getting Started with Seed Beads, 2007, by Dustin Wedekind
Jean Power's Geometric Beadwork, 2012, Jean Power
Suzanne Golden Presents, 2012, by Suzanne Golden

Introduction for Backwards Readers

I always begin at the back of a book, and I never follow directions. I suspect the two are related. If you're like me, you'll love that *Contemporary Geometric Beadwork* isn't about following patterns, it's about exploring ideas. We've tried to be crystal clear about the basics, and we've given long, full patterns when we thought we needed to, but it's no secret that we have explorer's hearts, and rarely repeat.

There was so much that we meant to stuff into this book. When we first dreamed it up, Dustin and I were making discs and Cones and flowers and spirals (see photo above), and then Jean Power came on board, bringing her exciting shapes and forms, and before we knew it we had over 400 pages of OMG, we had wandered away from all flat work, and we knew that unless we were planning on building an encyclopedia set, we needed a new way of making it all happen.

We split Jean's body of work off into a separate volume that she masterminded, and it was published in Fall of 2012 as *Jean Power's Geometric Beadwork,* and you can find it (and Jean) at **www.jeanpower.com**.

We weren't so worried about size after that, as we knew that *CGB* would also be an eBook, capable of holding worlds within worlds of information, links to photos and extra galleries, live links to artists and their blogs and shops and kits and web sites. We could build a live Index and Resources section. With that kind of depth on our side, we began rustling trees all over the world, publishing our ideas on our web sites and Facebook page, seeing what people would make.

It was clear that the exploration of the ideas on our table could be a life's-work. No matter how much time we spent making and thinking, there would still be an infinite number of forms left to build. In truth, they already exist, because the mathematical combinations that would result in those new shapes exist without effort, interference or calculation on our part; they simply are. We can build them or not build them, but we do not affect their capacity to exist. I could model them with a computer and make some real headway, but I could never make them all with my hands. It was exciting for me when Christina joined the team, as she was as interested in the math as I was.

It was very freeing to give away our ideas instead of protecting them, because it was only a confirmation of my belief that there are enough ideas for everyone; why not include as many hands in the book as possible? The results of our open format exceeded anything I could have dreamed.

Our approach has been unusual, to say the least, but look how well it worked to channel Harry Truman, who said, "It's amazing what you can accomplish if you don't care who gets the credit." Although we've tried to be as scrupulous as we could about who did what when, this has been a true community project, and advances and ideas have come from everyone who participated. And that's a fact.

Two views of a beaded orange plastic toy gun by Jeroen Medema. It's a project he began at the original Seed Bead Summit.

(We bead in peace.)

What's coming in Volume II?

Besides more more more Winging and Horning and Zigging and Zagging and Coning and Helixing? Geometric Chains and Ropes, of course, and definitely more mixed media. Look for handmade metal parts to make their entry into the mix...

Above, Cate Jones' ruffled purple *Sixagon Chain*, and above right, JoAnn Baumann's interpretation in colourful seed beads. Below, Gabriella van Diepen's beautiful *Geometric Puff Rope*, waiting for a metal and chain frame that Kate can't wait to build.

Pentagons bewitch us, and they're on our list to fully explore. There are several of them in Gabriella's rope, opposite, and below, you can see two stunning examples of Jean Power's Pentagon Bangle pattern, expertly rendered in 15° Delica cylinders by Lia Melia. Photo by Kyle Cassidy.

Contemporary Geometric Beadwork by Kate McKinnon 235

Teresa Sullivan's *Snake-Eye Puffs* intrigue us with their stiffness and undulating pattern. We're eager to explore ropes with seed beads as well as cylinders.

Below: a Funnel-Web Disc in circular square stitch on a beaded choker with a handmade fine silver clasp. Beadwork, Dustin Wedekind and Kate McKinnon, clasp forged by Kate, and the handmade glass bead was made by Joyce Rooks.

"Shadow is a colour as light is, but less brilliant; light and shadow are only the relation of two tones."

Paul Cézanne

"When we try to pick out anything by itself, we find it hitched to everything else in the universe."

John Muir

During the making of the book, several interesting pieces turned up that really turned us on.

ElJean Wilson's incredible peyote bracelet, above, had to be held to be fully appreciated. It featured a flat fabric of soft peyote stitch, a border of cubic right angle weave, and little peyote tubes that sat slightly above the fabric. You could slip a ribbon under them, or roll up little notes or prayers and slip them into the tubes.

In 2012, Jean Power was one of Beadwork Magazine's Designers of the Year, and one of the projects she dreamed up was her Heroine necklace, modelled at right by Gabriella van Diepen. If you make a Tri-Wing Ring, and zip the edges together, you can make 3-D triangles like this, for bangles or for chain. See Jean's magazine project for details of her focal.

Photo of Gabri by Kyle Cassidy.

These two pages, Delica Bead colours used in the book, listed by Miuyki number. Please see the eBook for the 23 elusive bead colours we weren't able to photograph.

240 Contemporary Geometric Beadwork by Kate McKinnon

Tables by Francesca Watson, photos courtesy of www.FireMountainGems.com.

Above: Dustin Wedekind and Teresa Sullivan at the start of it all, our first Seed Bead Summit in Tucson, Arizona, in May of 2011. Just out of frame are Jean Power, Marcia DeCoster, Gabriella van Diepen, Jeroen Medema and Kate McKinnon.

Opposite top: Jeroen Medema, Kyle Cassidy and Gabriella van Diepen

Right: Kyle and Jean Power
Below: Christina Vandervlist